SOLDIER OF GOOD FORTUNE

SOLDIER OF GOOD FORTUNE

JAMES BASS

This edition first published in 2014 by:

Thistle Publishing
36 Great Smith Street
London
SW1P 3BU

www.thistlepublishing.co.uk

ISBN-13: 978-1-910198-26-1

In memory of my
Grandfather James Barton
Bass 1897 - 1979

My Grandfather was a good and proud man, with a stubborn streak in him, you will realise that in this book. His story also shows how lucky he was. I wish he were alive today, as there are many questions I would ask him about the hardship and suffering soldiers had to endure throughout the Great War. He never spoke to me about the war and to be honest, I never asked, probably because I was only young and not really aware of his involvement. It was only 10 years ago that I found out about the memoirs he had written for my parents and on reading it I just had to put it into book form for the future. Over the last 7 years I have visited some of the places mentioned.

Kurt Barry Mayfield

PREFACE BY JAMES BASS

This book is dedicated to my daughter Margaret and son-in-law Barry Mayfield, at whose request it was written. It is a short record of my services in the Great War 1914 – 1918. A simple catalogue of my movements and experiences from the outbreak of war in 1914, when I had no hope of enlisting, my disappointment at that, and my desperate efforts to get myself up to the required standard when still underage.

Eventually I joined the City of London Rifles and went to war, taking part in several battles. I was taken prisoner in 1917 during a German counterattack in the battle of Cambria, ending with my escape to Bruxelles and being sheltered by Mademoiselle Anna Van Dael, a former nurse and member of Miss Edith Cavell's organisation to aid the escape of allied prisoners into Holland.

There are no exaggeration, no heroics, and no histrionics. The libraries are full of good books by experts telling of the great battles, the conditions in which the troops lived and fought.

The things I now tell have been my secrets through the years

James Barton Bass

CHAPTER ONE
IN THE BEGINNING

When war broke out on 4th August 1914, I was 17 years and 1 month. Being small I eyed the large recruiting poster in dismay! At that time the requirements were very selective, so I had to look elsewhere for some outlet for my patriotic ardour, whilst improving my physique.

The opportunity came when on September 6th I joined the Wandsworth Volunteer Training Corps, which operated chiefly around Wimbledon Common and Putney Heath. When the weather permitted I would rise very early, walk 2.5 miles to Queensmere on the Common for a swim, or alternatively take vigorous physical exercise and cold baths. There were Sunday morning boxing sessions under the guidance of Jaggers, the once famous London messenger boy.

I had the opportunity to master long distance walking, as a friend and neighbour was a member of the local walking club. but I benefited from it when the time came for marching in full kit on cobble roads. 'Walk from the hips' I was told, 'it's what is known as the Dutch Roll'.

I ate meat by the pound (I believe it was 2 pence a pound in those days) Two dinners each day and pints of milk. I worked fanatically until I came up to the required physical standard, except for the minimum age limit, which was 19.

It was in May 1915 when I decided to try my luck. First I went to the artillery establishment in Stratford in London's East End. I failed, despite a difference of opinion between two recruiters, not because of age, but that they finally considered I was not 'thick enough round the waist'.

From there I went to Farrington Road in the City, where I swore I was 19 and joined the 6th Battalion London Regiment 'City of London Rifles, 'the Cast Iron 6th'

(I am sure this was the same for many young impressionable lads, you hear some stories of some as young as 15 managing to sign up. **KBM**). I was issued with a uniform, puttees and boots, packed my suit and bowler in to a kit bag and walked the 7 miles home as proud as Punch. On my arrival home, my father, who, in spite of the threat that if I enlisted he would have me out, surrendered gracefully with the remark 'you silly fool'

The Battalion had rapidly reached 1,300 in strength.

In March the 1st Battalion had left with the 47th London Division, which with the 46th Midland Division, were the first two T.A. Divisions to join the army in France. There was such an overflow of recruits, that a second battalion was quickly formed and as with the first battalion, in August 1914, marched away to camps. The war office had finally issued orders that the T.A. units would be accepted for Imperial service provided that 90% volunteered for it. This was easily obtained and in a few weeks the last battalion marched to Bisley where a concentration camp was established.

When the 1st Battalion marched away there was an immediate flood of recruits, 1,100 attended as necessary forms were completed. The second Battalion was formed and destined for active service becoming part of the 58th London Division. Comprising the second line of units of the first twelve Battalions of the London Regiment (the London Regiment during the war raised 88 Battalions). The second Battalion went to East Anglia as part of the east coastal defence, and in January 1917 after concentrating at Sutton Veny, near Warminster left for France with the 58th Division.

Chapter Two
Training - Summer 1915

Meanwhile in March 1915, a 3rd battalion was raised to fill the gaps caused by casualties overseas. This battalion was formed into two large companies, which on alternate days would march to either Regents Park or Victoria Park for training. It was led by our BERSAGLIERI BAND (the only one in the British Army) consisting of 1 key bugle and 8 deep drums, as used by the Italian sharpshooters. The instruments were presented by the Italian community which inhabited Saffron Hill in the neighbourhood of Farringdon Road.

We had no equipment, but wore our great coats, rolled and tied at either end and worn bandolier fashion. It was great fun marching through the city streets. The servants came out on the balconies of large houses, cheering and throwing chocolate and cigarettes. The majority of us must have lived in the London area for we all went home at night.

When the battalion was furnished with sufficient NCO's, Non Commissioned Officers and Officers, off they marched to Hurst Park Race Course, I was already there with the advance party. What a fine sight to see the band and battalion crossing Hampton Court Bridge.

We were billeted in the race course stand, my company, B Company. in the outbuildings and A Company was across the road in the stables. The sergeant's mess claimed the Royal Box. This time we had equipment, but no rifles and khaki and underclothing were almost unobtainable. The 50 old, long .303 Lee Enfield rifles possessed were only to be used for musketry courses at Pirbright.

Here we were introduced to a 'remarkable man' our adjutant, Captain Clay M.B.E., a regular of many years service in the K.R.R. corps (Kings Royal Rifle Corps). He joined the battalion in 1906 as R.S.M (Regimental Sergeant Major) and after serving in the first battalion in France as R.S.M. returned to England in August 1915 expressly to build and maintain a draft finding unit of the highest efficiency and finest morale, which he did having the finest qualities for the task.

He was a disciplinarian, with a high pitched staccato voice, which delivered orders in a manner which made one keen to obey. I never heard him abuse anyone. He was understood and admired for what we knew he was trying to accomplish.

It was a hot summer with much time to enjoy it. The ambition was to become a man, enjoying their fitness, roughing it and as expected learning to smoke a pipe. It was a happy time, never to be equalled.

The first thing I let myself in for was a marathon, go as you please, race in full equipment, borrowed rifle and ammunition. Each platoon furnished a team of about 10 and left at regular intervals. Each team was timed on arrival. My team arrived in the second best time. As a kit inspection was necessary we incurred a penalty, as one of our team had forgotten his 'housewife' (sewing kit) which relegated our team to third place, nevertheless it was great fun.

We had Sports days for the amusement of relatives who journeyed down. It was through this that I become friendly with Ben Roberts from the Argentine. Ben taught me how to hurdle. I also became attached to Harry Norcott who joined the same time as me, at the age of 16, but he was very tall and looked older. Harry's home was at Windsor and the Thames his playground. He had become an accomplished oarsman (after the war he sculled for London Transport). I soon became pretty good at it, learning to feather my oars, skimming the water without a splash. Evening rows to

Kingston, returning when the houseboats were alive with coloured lights. There was also much swimming in the river.

When parents and friends were not visiting, it was off on the train to London for some entertainment.

One day I found myself with a party off to Onger in Essex for trench digging. It was rather dull here, except for a hot bath with strong disinfectant at the workhouse and seeing the Zeppelin brought down in flames at Potters Bar there was little to pass the time.

One Sunday at Hurst Park something occurred which is probably unique in the annals of the British Army, or it would have been had it not been hushed up. This fine morning we marched off to a Service at East Molesey. On the way back uppermost in our thoughts was a quick lunch and an afternoon at home or by the river with friends or relatives. At the dismissal we found the battalion was confined to barracks. There was no reason given and no one had any idea what for, whatever the reason it occurred at the top and to this day to me has remained a mystery. Major Stokes was at this time in command and he was a hated by the men. I only remember seeing him on the one occasion, but knew of his bad reputation. My guess is that Major Stokes had had some disagreement with his fellow officers, which occasioned him to show his authority and being spiteful by nature, was willing to deprive 1300 innocents of a beautiful summer afternoon's enjoyment.

We sat down for the midday meal, for which for some reason was delayed, which only caused dissatisfaction to increase. Groups were seated outdoors undercover. The protest began, more in fun, at one of the tables. A chant of 'We will not be confined to barracks' accompanied by knives and forks drummed in rhythm, was quickly taken up by other tables, until increasing in volume, it echoed around the racecourse buildings, as anger began to show. The meal over and time for freedom arrived, the lads gathered in groups. They were bewildered and unsure what to do and had no one to explain and give advice until Sgt Major Phillips appeared. He was surrounded by a crowd wanting to know what it was all about, 'what were we to do? 'they asked. Choosing his words carefully, so not to commit himself 'I know what I would do, if I were you' looking towards the main gate. Need he have said more. The hint taken, there was a mass of movement for the gate. I was in the front rank as Captain Macdonald appeared from nowhere, flinging his arms wide in front appealing for calm as we spilled out onto the towpath and away home.

At the appointed time that night every man had returned, not one absentee, to the great credit of the 1300 concerned and not a mention of what had begun some 9 hours earlier, it was as though nothing had happened. What was without any doubt a serious incident, shrouded in mystery, was quickly forgotten.

October came and conditions at Hurst Park became unfavourable, so Surbiton opened its hearts and homes to us. The disadvantage was the troops were scattered and facilities for training inadequate, which meant a 3 mile march each day to Esher Common before any drill.

I was billeted at No 1 Surbiton road, near old Father Thames. It was the home of a middle aged widow, who did everything to make life pleasant for us. There were four of us, all under aged. A maid in her middle twenties lived in. Her name was Nelly, and we teased her shamefully.

One day we decided we would frighten her on the following morning. According to plan, when she came into the room we made as if to leap out of bed and collar her, she fled with a scream. From then onwards she would only venture her head round the door frame.

We were four very innocent young lads, having what we saw as innocent fun. I can remember one more occasion when we thought to scare poor Nell. We were always up to bed about ten and Nell came up soon after. Her bedroom was on the landing four stairs below. Giving her time to get comfortable, one of us (guess who?) rolled a boot – thump-thump-thump, down the stairs and we heard her rush to her room door and lock it. Sadly two of the four met their untimely deaths a few months later, one missing and believed killed, the other blown to fragments before my very eyes.

I am eternally grateful to Nell, who during the awful years was my guiding star, my mentor and my inspiration. She was unfortunately that much older than me. We exchanged constant lengthy letters and I drew many comical cartoons for her. It was a sad day; when after the war, parting was inevitable, but nothing will ever destroy the goodness I felt from her.

Christmas 1915, was the last Christmas at home until 1918. It was the last time I saw my home until October 1917 (twenty two months later). In January when we entrained for Wiltshire, the good people of Surbiton turned out in force to cheer us on our way.

Now in Fovant and Salisbury Plain, winter was a far different kettle of fish. There were seven London Battalions in hutments here on the slope opposite Compton Down, where our badges in chalk were later to appear.

Our battalion, the 6th, worked at the top next to the parade ground. The huts went down to the main highway and roads were made between them. After the heavy snow melted, thousands of boots churned the earth into deep liquid slosh, requiring much labour with shovels and zinc baths.

Whilst the snow lay thick, the London Rifle Brigade, who occupied the lowest huts by the road, came up to raid us with snowballs. Quickly alerted we took up positions on the parade ground. Assisted by snowball makers, who brought up loads of ammunition in wheelbarrows, we in the front line soon routed the L.R.B's, who hurriedly returned to their huts.

We had to teach the LRB's a real lesson, and they would surely now be between the blankets, although it was not yet lights out. We 'cased' the chosen hut and found the occupants either in, or preparing for bed. The small top windows were open, and below each window a man was posted, snowballs at the ready, similarly, a man at the doors at each end of the hut. At the agreed signal both doors were opened and the snowballs poured in. At the same time more poured in through windows on to the beds, and we disappeared silently into the night.

One fine crisp Sunday afternoon, with the snow almost gone, myself, Caddick, Cox and Chilman, who had become inseparable, decided to visit a small isolated village where we heard the inhabitants welcomed visitors and one could expect a nice cup of tea. So we climbed Compton Down and made our way as best we could in the direction of the village. It was not easy, for up there on the Down was featureless and had only sheep tracks, which criss-crossed, turned and twisted, a regular maze. However, we managed to find a way which brought us to a short sunken road and there were the cottages. Knocking at the first door we were invited in as though we were expected. It was great to be in a home once more with its cosy warmth and amongst people who were interested in the young boys who would soon be 'over there '

By the time we had had tea, the oil lamp was lit and soon the darkness descended without our being aware of it. When we were leaving the front door opened and to our astonishment, we could see nothing but a blanket of deep snow. This caused us some concern remembering our difficult journey to reach there. As we walked, we could only see only some twenty yards ahead of us. There was nothing for it but to keep going. We plunged on, in what we hoped was a straight course, stopping occasionally and looking around into the darkness. I have no idea how long we travelled, but I was in good company, we made light of our plight, even recognising the possibility of spending the night, goodness knows how, in the open.

We were brought to halt suddenly by what at first appeared to be a thousand bright stars. We found we were standing on the edge of the Down with lights appearing to be hanging in mid air. The snow obliterated everything else. It must have taken a little time to realise these hanging lights were the electric light bulbs from the huts. We could not see on the opposite slope. I could not believe our good fortune. We could have landed anywhere and even then not been able to know where we were, but by some uncanny means came right to the spot where we had started our climb to the top.

We were a happy quartet; Joe Caddick was a born comedian, who kept us in fits. He would, apparently unconscious of our presence, walk round and round the inside of a hut facing the walls and in a quiet voice engage in an impromptu conversation with an imaginary person. I have sometimes listened to a child walk round the walls talking to someone who was not there, but to me Joe's efforts were sheer genius.

Unfortunately, the time was approaching when we would be parted, and wherever my three partners went, I know they survived, but I have never seen them again. Still their memory lingers on; Joe Caddick became a lance corporal and gained a Military Medal, as did Chilman, who became a corporal. Cox is not in our roll of honour, so evidently he survived, so we all came through.

At last we were armed, although, still the old long .303 Lee Enfields. We soon realized that this was the toughening up period. (They must have realised that the school boy fun and games were now over and that reality was about to hit them. **KBM**) It became more and more evident that some of us would soon be needed to fill some of the gaps caused by casualties in our 1st Battalion. Training was speeded up with bayonet drill for the first time. This was the first time I fired a rifle on the range there, I cannot say I ever saw a bull's eye, being as I was a little short sighted, but somehow I passed. With this I soon found I was in one of two drafts. In February the date was fixed, my draft was the first to go. The CO. (Commanding Officer) inspected us, scrutinizing us most thoroughly. I am certain he was aware that many were there under false pretences, being under the age for active service. He stood before me in doubt. 'how old are you,' '19 sir,' 'are you sure'? 'Yes sir. 'you know what will happen to you if you get out there and it is found you are under age,' 'Yes sir' I replied. I had no idea what would and I didn't give a darn.

Next morning arrived and our CSM (Company Sergeant Major), who had been wounded at Festubert and walked with a stiff leg, said goodbye to 'his boys', in real tears. The train whisked us away to Southampton and we boarded a darkened ship at night and departed with a Destroyer escort.

We landed at Le Havre in a strange land; tents were everywhere, with troops of all regiments. Every morning, led by a piper, we went up to the bullring, where we did all sorts of silly things, like dashing about in those horrible stocking gas helmets which caused the eye pieces to steam up (we looked like bank robbers).

I remember Le Harve chiefly for the mattresses hanging over the balconies in the morning, the perpetual stink of incinerators and the revelation of the inhumane treatment by the French of their work horses, many of which, throughout our life in France, we saw working with sores being chafed by the harness.

Isn't it strange, we had been moulded into a very smart and proficient unit, but, we had been taught nothing of trench warfare, in consequence of which, what we were about to receive came as a great shock to us, but fortunately, our pride sustained us, and we were quick to learn. So off we went WAR.

Chapter Three
France 1916

The Zuave Valley And Mining Activity On Vimy Ridge

In the honours list, of the 47th London Divisions is one for the 'German attack on Vimy ridge'. During Christmas and there-after, the line that we had taken over from the French was held by Saxons, and had been a quiet period, but could have been so planned to mask the tunnelling which later developed into mining. The advantage was with the enemy, who had excellent observation in all directions. On the opposite side of the valley and the two rivers, the Souchez and Carency, was the Lorrette Heights which was in British hands.

On the downward slope to the La Basse – Arras road and behind our front lines lay the Zuave valley along which the Germans could put down an almost impassable barrage. Communications were never reliable in the valley as most was hidden from German observation, and therefore was often visited with very heavy fire, chiefly Howitzers. During the heavy fighting it could not even be crossed by runners. The mining activity on the ridge opened on the 20th April when the enemy exploded 2 great mines beneath the 25th Division which was on the right of the 47th.

Similar activity was expected on our front, held by the 19th London Regiment, therefore, my Company, went up to support them. No sooner were we in position than a mine exploded demolishing the front line, and making a crater 40ft across. After a short silence the usual heavy bombardment and the struggle for the crater began. I had no knowledge of the evil reputation of the Zuave valley at this time, but I was about to experience it.

Our platoon Sgt called for volunteers to fetch ammunition. Being the nearest to him I obliged, and was joined by Jones, Jonas, Mynott and L/Cpl Jackson who took charge. We descended the communication trench which overlooked the lower ground of the Souchez valley. On our way we passed a dugout which had just been hit and was still smoking. It was Company HQ. We learned later that our CSM Diggins had been killed. The trench from here was severely damaged, and as we neared the Zuave valley it was almost obliterated, denying us any protection. We managed to cross safely and collected our boxes, but the return crossing was a very hazardous undertaking with short dashes, diving down full length, crawling and dragging the boxes. It almost seemed impossible to get through alive, but we did, and reaching shelter we lay panting.

Shortly after this L/Cpl Jackson was awarded the DCM for returning a German grenade which fell into the trench, thereby saving many lives.

We were very fortunate at this time to have the support of batteries of French 75's. Our artillery had not the strength of the enemy at this stage (we were still minus steel helmets and gumboots) and it was a joy to hear the distinctive rapid bark of our 'soixante-quinze' (French 75mm Field Gun). This intensive mining period which continued from April 20th to May 15th was nerve wracking for men holding the forward trenches, as no one could be certain he was not standing above a volcano ready to erupt. It was an awful feeling.

There was an enemy mine on the 26th April and one of ours on the 29th. Two of the enemies sprung on the 30th, between two former craters, demolished the whole of the company's front line and caused us 80 casualties. This one was named 'Mildren Crater' after our commanding officer.

Eleven enemy galleries were suspected just south, and there was great activity by our tunnelers. The result of this feverish activity was that 4 mines were sprung beneath the enemy lines.

I well remember the urgency, the 8 hour candles down the tunnel, the man sitting at the entrance busy extracting the hot foul air by means of a semi-rotary pump. Care had to be exercised where the earth bags were dumped, so not to indicate where the gallery was.

To conclude we had the last word, as on the 15th May we put up another string of mines.

Going back to 30th April, when at 6.45pm two large mines were sprung under our front line. Enemy fire continued for two hours, concentration on communications trenches was severely heavy and all telephone wires were cut. Rifleman Murphy volunteered to take a message to Battalion HQ, although he was never expected to reach his destination, he not only did so but returned and collapsed through sheer exhaustion, for which he received the MM, Military Medal.

It was no wonder we re-named the Zuave valley, 'death valley'. On the evening of the 29th, at 'stand to', my bombing section was posted in Rabineau Trench, which ran from immediate support a short distance to the front line. I was standing behind the rest, in the junction of the two trenches. The two enemy mines, already mentioned, were fired under our front line, ahead of Rabineau Trench. The earth rocked, Rabineau Trench collapsed and buried many friends. I only escaped because I was stood in the intersection. The heat from the blast struck my face and I saw the huge red ball of fire emerge slowly from the earth, and rising, disappeared in black smoke. I was scarcely aware of the attempt to dig out my friends, as I was whisked away to rush boxes of grenades up to the area of the craters where a fierce struggle was in progress to gain the far lip of the crater. Our lads were standing on top throwing as quickly as possible, the noise and flashes were terrific.

When relieved after the first experience, we retired to the huge French huts in Bouvigny Woods on Lorrette Heights. We were all bedded down when in came our Company Commander, Captain Maynard (as he was then). He praised us for our behaviour in difficult and testing circumstances and began to name the comrades we had lost, but he was so overcome he had to wipe away the tears.

All this frenzied activity was a prelude to the German attack on 21st May. This was still the age of the rifle. The Vickers machine gun was prominent in the front line. The gunners at night greeted the enemy gunners with a 'rat a tat-tat-tat' and received the same in reply. Little excuse was needed to start an outburst of rapid fire along our frontline. This soon would be the end of that sort of warfare, where one could step from communication trenches into country and civilians. The change was still two months away where miles of country villages, trees and roads would be obliterated, and the big guns never silent for over four months.

I was still underage, and could if I wished, be sent home, but the comradeship was too strong, and I had always been fascinated by war since I was able to read. We boys believed the British soldier to be invincible. I got great satisfaction copying maps showing positions during past battles, and drawing pictures of our heroes such as Marlborough, Wolfe of Quebec, Clive of India and Wellington. My family home was about 200yds from Nelson's house, Merton place.

An example of what my comrades were like occurred one night during an alarm. I found myself and a friend, Bill West, being sent from the immediate support trench to the front line. After standing down in the morning we were returning to our support position, when we met a Sergeant, who, to my surprise, said to my friend 'here, you are wounded, have the wound dressed at once.' He had a gunshot wound in the upper arm which he had concealed from me. I had been with him through the night and he had said nothing.

Along the valley of the Souchez and Carency was ample evidence of the advance by the French the previous September. Wherever we re-dug old trenches, we found French and German corpses had been thrown in and buried. One could identify the Germans by their leather valises with animal hair on and the dugouts on the Lorrette Heights, which we took over from the French, were decorated over the entrances with human skulls.

When I visited Vimy with the British Legions epic pilgrimage in 1928, I spent a whole day on the ridge. Across the valley I could see, on Lorrette, the white lighthouse built by the French Nation to guide home the spirits of the fallen. Every night it flashed its message over a radius of many miles. A ceremony was held there in memory of 110,000 French who gave their lives on and around Lorrette in the terrible fighting of 1914 and 1915. There is also a memorial church and cemetery containing 4,000 graves. In the Ossuary there are tiers and tiers of ebony coffins containing bones and skulls picked up on the battlefield that are surrounded by lamps which shine night and day. I have read that Lorrette is the 'eye of Artois' (Artois a former province in France between Flanders and Picardy with Arras as its capital) and that whoever could hold Vimy, would win the war.

Owing to the heavy fire the enemy could concentrate on communications, it often caused long delays in bringing up the rations. The weather turned very hot at Easter and (according to my notes) the rations were delayed for a few days, and thirst became a problem. I can remember this well, as I had just received a parcel containing a bottle of Worcester sauce that I had requested. It tasted like wine and I was pestered to hand out swigs.

In the trench I was in, on the low ground, there was an 2ft. square exit in the parados at ground level through which one could crawl (the trench was built up from ground level). Lying on the ground and looking, a shell hole was seen which was full of very murky water. Those on the spot filled water bottles. On a subsequent visit to this position, when by this time the heat had dried the water up, the shell hole was found to contain a skeleton.

Our way out of the line to the road at Villers-au-Bois, was always done by night at high speed. It was some 3 miles of communication trench. Round and round the bays and the devil take the hindmost, to arrive dead beat, and in need of water.

CHAPTER FOUR
21ST MAY 1916

France
German Attack On Vimy Ridge –
Western Slope Of Northern Spur

After the intensive struggle during a month of feverish mining, the enemy failed to blow us from our front line and immediate support trenches, owing to the counter mining by our Royal Engineers, assisted nightly by troops brought up to help with the tunnelling, and who worked from old French listening galleries.

According to intelligence captured, 650 pieces of heavy artillery were brought up, and placed unobserved, in order for the attack to be made with complete surprise. In this they succeeded.

The main direction of the attack was against the front overlooking the Zuave valley. The 47th London Division had relieved the 25th Division on our right, which had been blown out of their front line. They recovered it by counter-mining. It was these two Divisions which were attacked. From the 15th May the enemy began his preparation by demolishing the front trenches and reducing the garrisons. Our front (47th Division), which had been left by the 25th Division in a very poor state of defence, was held by disconnected posts, isolated by day. No shelter at all in the front system.

On the 21st May the enemy guns started early. At 3.30pm the bombardment became intense, and a 'box barrage' on the Zuave valley cut all communications. The trenches were pounded mercilessly, and the troops, especially in the shelterless trenches, suffered terribly. At 7.45pm the shelling lifted from the front trenches and fell with increased violence on the Zuave valley.

With this the Germans came over in great force, and our 7th Battalion (Shiny Seventh) and 8th Battalion (Post Office Rifles) who had lain for 4 hours in unprotected trenches, were driven from the front line, across two supports, into a line half way down the slope. The 7th made a local counter attack at 8.40pm, but had not sufficient strength to recapture any ground. This led to much confusion. Battalion Commanders found it impossible to coordinate counter attacks. Briefly, what followed resembled a game of chess.

Company Commanders had to employ great initiative. Counter attacking with platoons, searching for troops on either flank, filling the gaps, doing everything to deny to the enemy the Zuave valley, which would give him observation of our rear and which would have meant abandoning that part of the ridge. During this time, our Divisional artillery was in the process of changing over, so the infantry had little or no support. My company was in support at the 'Cabaret Rouge', on the La Bassee – Arras road. It was daylight when the order to 'fall in' came. We tumbled out of our dugouts on to the road. Although the 'Cabaret Rouge' was under bombardment, we stood in ranks whilst the roll was called. I remember a shell falling into a large corrugated iron latrine, in the open behind us, scattering it in all directions.

We proceeded in single file up the slope. On the way our CQM (Chief quarter master) and another, handed to each of us a linen bandolier of ammunition, remarking continually 'give them hell lads'. In the end the enemy were halted short of their objective. Our artillery at last joined in, and after much counter attacking in small groups, with bayonets, and bomb, they were pushed back and both sides had to dig-in afresh.

In four days it was over, and the north spur of Vimy Ridge remained in British hands until the capture of the whole ridge by the brave Canadians in the following April 1917.

On being relieved the Division marched back to Bruay, a large town, where we were soon engaged in emptying dustbins and sweeping the streets, no doubt in preparation for the visit of the Lord Mayor of London. During his visit the decorations won in the recent battle were distributed. The large number of recipients give an indication of the heroism displayed by the men of the London Division, and in particular my Regiment, the 6th London Regiment, City of London Rifles, which received two MC, Military Crosses, five DCM's, Distinguished Conduct Medal, and eight MM, Military Medals.

On 12th June the Battalion moved back to the line, taking over no.1 sector at Souchez, where the trenches were water-logged. Its was very unpleasant to step off the road into water which soon filled ones boots, and how it squelched as we walked. These conditions would be endured for a week before an opportunity came to take off our boots. The result of this was severe waterbite. The soles of the feet became white, bloodless and corrugated, like my mothers hands used to get after a mornings washing. On one occasion, on being relieved, and getting on to the hard road, I had lost the use of my legs so much, that I could not march with the others. I had to find my own way, in my own time, back to billets, where I found the cooks preparing breakfast. They welcomed me with a mug of tea and a tot of rum. After breakfast it was 'boots off 'and expose the feet to the air and sunlight.

We were now on low ground, and changed about between four Sectors. In one of these sectors tapping and picking could be heard, and tunnelling beneath us was suspected, so the R.E's (Royal Engineers) sprung a mine to put a stop to that.

There were three raids by the Division in the first month since June 12th. The ASC brought up 1,300 gas cylinders in GS wagons, with old motor tyres fitted to the wheels, to be discharged preceding the first raid. What a difficult, awkward job carrying these cylinders up to the communication trench, as they had to be tilted to get them round each traverse. The second raid wasn't as successful as the first. The enemy put down a box barrage, this failed to trap the raiders, but kept them from getting nearer than bombing distance. During the raid our Brigade trench mortar battery, fired 750 rounds in half an hour. The third raid was in 2 parts. The first party found no Germans in the trench. A few hours later a second party followed, and was met with all kinds of fire. Only a few reached and bombed the trench. It was later learnt that the enemy frequently overheard telephone messages on their listening sets. When this was finally realized, many things adopted fancy names. At this time a few 'fullerphones' were issued for the first time to Divisions. These telegraph instruments defy listening sets.

I was in the front line in one of these Sectors, the enemy front line was so close here that one evening at 'stand to' I saw and heard Ben Millett, who spoke good German, holding a conversation with the enemy opposite.

An incident occurred about this time when a ration party returned one night. One, Kushner, a Polish Jew, and not very popular, being a 'windy' type, thought he would be clever enough to pick up a jar of rum. He prepared to indulge, whilst dashing all hopes of anyone sharing. He took a swig, and spat it out in a hurry, for it was Vermeil spray, which was used for spraying trenches after receiving poison gas. He did look silly.

Apart from the raids it was fairly quiet during June and July.

Meanwhile, the Royal Naval Division had been learning the ways of war on the Western Front from us (after their Gallipoli experience). It was strange to see these bearded men with names like 'Drake' on their arm. Once, whilst talking to some of them, a German plane crashed a few yards away. Quick as a flash one of them whipped off the dead pilot's fur lined thigh boots, just in time to avoid the enemy artillery fire which was quickly brought to bear, in order to destroy the aircraft.

Experience on Vimy Ridge had taught us to arrange our defences in greater depth. At the very end of July we handed over to the RN Division, and began our long trek to Abbeville and from there to the Somme.

I would like to point out the contempt shown by the infantry, at this period, towards those who enjoyed comfortable conditions behind the front line. The MT, ASC came in for the majority of it. Marching from the forward area to reserve huts, on the road after some six miles, we always came upon a group of ASC personnel sitting at tables outside an isolated estaminet drinking and chatting up the French maidens. This always incensed the infantry lads who would sing, with venom, 'we are Fred Karno's army, the MT ASC, we cannot fight, we cannot ****, what bloody good are we, etc'. (A nickname applied to the new British army raised during the war in allusion to Fred Karno, the comedian and producer of stage burlesque) This was quickly forgotten after the tragic July 1st, after which everyone was in the fray.

CHAPTER FIVE
SEPTEMBER 15ᵀᴴ 1916

France
The Somme – Battle Of High Wood

In almost tropical heat the Division set forth upon the trek through the lush Picardy countryside on the 1ˢᵗ August 1916. The first day it was agony, feet had to harden after long spells in waterlogged trenches. However, after the first few days, marching commenced soon after dawn and ended in time for a midday meal. The cobbled roads made marching more difficult, but who cared. Beautiful weather, lovely country, fresh country bread, butter, milk and eggs from the farms. It was much cooler at night to sleep under an apple tree or in the farmers trap. Eventually we arrived at Millencourt, near Abbeville. Here we stayed for a fortnight in splendid relaxation, with occasional practice attacks.

On the 20ᵗʰ August, with regret, we left Millencourt, and after three nights rest reached Franvillers on the 23ʳᵈ. Step by step, nearing the 'melting pot', where every unit of the army was to take part. When our Division finally up, pulled out, the final casualties for the battle were to reach 22,923 officers and 476,553 other ranks, compared with the German figures of 444,933 all ranks.

Someplace before Franvillers we had our first ration of margarine. It came in large tins and I didn't like it one bit.

On the journey along the river Somme we spent a night in a village, where a river ran through the centre, with a bridge connecting the two halves. In the afternoon I took my towel and set off along the bank to find a secluded spot for a swim. The river wasn't too wide, and the water came almost to the top of the bank. I entered the water unadorned, swimming up and down, round and round, until I had had enough. As I approached the edge to my alarm two young French maidens arrived on the scene, and began, amid titters, a cheeky conversation. I knew what I was in for. After a little more swimming, I decided, I was getting cold; I would have to pretend they weren't there. When they considered the show was over, they departed laughing and gesticulating.

At Franvillers we had another three weeks training for the attack and then on to Blackwood camp, where we watched Germans shells falling on Albert, sending up clouds of smoke. That evening they scattered the Scottish pipers playing retreat, and shells falling near the horse lines killed some mules. The next day we handed over our packs and fixed haversacks onto our backs. We marched up through Albert and saw the famous Virgin holding out her child as we passed beneath her. We spent the night near as Bazentin-Le-Petit in half dug trenches.

At dawn we heard a strange noise. It was the noise, so familiar today of tractors. There was a rush to investigate and we saw for the first time a few tanks moving up very slowly. I have forgotten all the names but one, the 'Crème de Menthe'. We imagined the shock Jerry was in for and there was great excitement. We little knew how these monsters were going to fail in their first attempt, and mess up the whole plan, causing great loss of life by preventing the troops that they were to assist, from getting the necessary artillery support. We had never seen anything like this place called 'High Wood' before. It had been attacked by the 47th Division on the 14th July unsuccessfully, as happened in subsequent assaults and was therefore holding up the third and last phase of the Somme battle. The front line the 47th Division took over and ran through the centre of this wood which was practically impenetrable, crowded as it was with ragged tree stumps, linked with barbed wire, sticking up from churned up earth, and a mass of corruption. The surrounding countryside was absolutely featureless, which was to cause more confusion as casualties mounted.

It was to be a three Corps affair. Our Division was to attack on the two Brigade front. Our Brigade the 140th on the right, joining up with the New Zealand Division, the 141st Brigade on our left, joining to its left, the 50th Division. Our Divisional front was roughly one mile wide.

The objectives of the 47th were –

1.   A line clear of High Wood, the Switch line
2.   The Starfish line, halfway down the forward slope. Here the direction turned a little to the left
3.   The strong Flers line, with the final objective a further mile and a half away

The plan for the 140th was for the 7th London to link with the New Zealanders on our right and the 15th London to work along the edge of the wood to suppress machine gun fire from concealed positions. They were to capture the first objective, the Switch line. This accomplished, the 8th London continued the advance passing through the 7th and 15th to take the Starfish line. The operation was to be completed by the 6th London assaulting the final objective, passing over the ground already taken by the other three battalions.

It was an uncomfortable night lying in an unfinished trench about 1ft. deep. Zero hour was at 6.30am. The troops attacking High Wood were at once engaged in heavy fighting. Four tanks went with the attack, but could make no headway. Broken tree stumps and deeply pitted ground barred the way and they could give no assistance, which deprived the much needed artillery support for the infantry. The 17th, 18th and half the 15th had to fight desperately for every foot of ground. Bombs, rifle fire and machine guns from undamaged concrete emplacements mowed them down. On the flanks the progress was faster. The 7th captured the Switch line, the 6th (my battalion) meanwhile had moved forward into its assembly position, and at 8.30am we were to get the ordered to advance. We were in good form. Our platoon officer, Lt Perry, handed out cigars, the guns intensified their fire, until, as one officer wrote 'the roar and explosions was almost more than human beings could stand'.

At the sound of the whistle we leapt from the trench, smoking our cigars and the cry of 'all berry 'rang out from my platoon. (The cry of 'all berry' comes from the London greengrocers selling holly and mistletoe at Christmas). We, the 6th, went forward on a 500yd frontage. Four waves, each wave composed of one platoon from each of the 4 Companies (my company linked with the New Zealanders), an interval of 100 yards between waves. Platoon Commanders accompanied 1st, 2nd and 4th waves. Company Commanders and CSM's, with the 3rd waves. At first the advance preceded like a drill movement until the broken and pitted ground made it difficult to keep formation, about this time the tank managed to get stuck near some of the 6th taking cover, and opened fire on the unfortunates. A Company Commander had a heated altercation with the tank commander who refused to take any further part in the battle.

It had become apparent that the 15th had failed to establish itself along the eastern side of High Wood and that the 8th were unable to get beyond the Switch line. Parties of the 8th had, with great dash, reached their objective, the Starfish line, but the advancing 6th met with stiff resistance from the German garrison. On the right the enemy rose from their trenches to meet the advancing waves in the open, and in the open they were slain.

Further on the right the New Zealanders were checked, so the enemy was able to concentrate on the 6th from both flanks. The gap caused by the failure of the 141st Brigade to take High Wood, had left our left flank and the right flank of the 50th Division wide open.

I was at first half aware of my friends falling to the ground, then something hit me a terrible blow, like the kick of a horse. The reaction sat me down with a jerk. Whilst I sat there, I remember L/Cpl White coming back from a wave in front, waving his hand and almost dancing with joy, for he had his single ticket to England. 'Can you see those fingers?' he said. When someone answered 'yes "you are a liar' he replied, 'cause they are not there', three fingers were missing. I will come back to myself again later.

It was now about 9am, what was happening to the 141st Brigade? High Wood was the key to the success of the battle and the enemy realized this too. So determined was their resistance that it was not before 1pm, after 6 hours continuous fighting that the wood was finally taken. Our losses here were very heavy. From this was establish a line clear of the wood. The attack was going on, but was endangered by the gap opposite High Wood. The 50th Division to our left had occupied to their 2nd objective, but their right flank was still exposed and they couldn't hold their ground.

Three battalions of the 142nd Brigade were sent forward leaving only one battalion in reserve. The 21st and 24th Battalions attacked the Starfish line, and captured Starfish redoubt, but their attempt to get on to the Cough Drop failed. The 24th Battalion, attacking from the wood could not reach the Starfish Line, but dug in 200 yards short.

The two battalion suffered fearfully, the 21st Battalion had only two officers and 60 ranks left unwounded, from 17 officers and 550 other ranks. Meanwhile the 6th Battalion unsupported from their left was receiving enfilade fire from the Cough Drop. This cluster of trenches and machine gun emplacements was allotted as a final objective of the 141st Brigade, but the heavy fire from this direction left the 6th Battalion no alternative but to deviate from its line of advance, not to avoid the Cough Drop, but to overcome it. It was captured mainly by my Company 'C', but not before the defenders had exacted a heavy toll of casualties from the Battalion. Remnants of out first wave reached their final objective, but were too few to form a permanent lodgement. The Battalion, for the time being, had to be content with the capture of the Cough Drop and taking prisoners.

At 6pm the 141st Brigade was still fighting for the 141st Brigades Starfish line objective. The field artillery had been brought up to High Wood and the night was spent in consolidating.

The battle went on. The Division continued the assault until 8th October, taking Le Sars and Eaucourt L'Abbaye, finishing at the front of the Butte de Warlencourt, some 3 ½ miles from the start. It is said that the 6th Battalion was relieved, 'weary to the point of exhaustion'. Press correspondents spoke of the final capture of High Wood as sharing with 'Verdun' the distinction of being the finest feat of the war'.

Let us now go back to the moment I found myself on the ground. I looked at myself expecting to see blood. I removed my equipment and undid my tunic, looking for a hole somewhere. Finding one in my trousers I went back to the tunic and there was a point of entry through the right hand pocket and I quickly realized I was carrying a grenade in each of my pockets. Gingerly, I put in my hand and brought it out. To my horror I found the nose cap and about 1/3 of the grenade missing, and by some miracle the detonator stood exposed and undamaged. I carefully hurled it to a safe distance.

I returned to investigate the hole. First taking out my first aid kit, I undid my trousers and found a hole in my right groin. There was not much bleeding, I doused it with iodine and as best I could, fixed a wad of lint over it. The bullet had gone right through the fob pocket, and smashed to pieces, a fine pair of nail scissors, which I had taken that morning from a German prisoner, some French coins and metal trouser buttons (there were more pieces inside me, but I was not aware of this at that moment). Now the next thing was to find my way to the Dressing Station, so I half stood up, looking round for some landmarks. I had to find my way back as best I could, but found myself veering too much to the right and crossing a trench full of New Zealanders. I decided to continue down a communication trench which was in good order and soon became deep. Round and round the traverses I went. I eventually located the Battalion headquarters dugout. Our Commanding Officer asked me where the Battalion was. I said I don't know.

There now seemed no danger from shell fire, and I judged myself to be out of machine gun range, so at the first opportunity I got up on top where I soon fell in with my old friend L/Cpl Wally Hancock.

As we walked along we became aware of bullets humming like bees round our feet. I assume they must have come from traversing fire from the edge of the wood which was still in enemy hands. Wally said 'what about a nice Blighty one?' (A term used by the British soldiers meaning a wound that would get you sent back to England. **KBM**). He was dancing about trying to get one, and sure enough, one went through the rear of his heel.

Hours later, at dusk, we staggered into Albert, joining a queue in the street, at the head of which Royal Army Medical Corps orderlies were dressing wounds as fast as they could. I heard a strange noise behind me, looking round, I saw an awful sight, a poor fellow with the whole of his lower jaw blown away, and he was trying to talk.

I was soon on a Red Cross train which arrived at Etaples and was taken to the Canadian hospital there. For several mornings they probed and extracted small pieces of scissors, coins and buttons from my groin.

At High Wood the weather broke and the land became a general morass, mud up to the axles of wheeled transport. After the 15th September, it was two weeks before a single mule truck got through over the High Wood crest. But the successful assault on the 15th and 16th September might have been much more, one Company Commander observed that the attack by the 6th Battalion and the surprise of a tank entering Flers (which was never seen again) was not exploited. There is little doubt, that had fresh troops been thrown in on the afternoon of the 15th, many months of weary of fighting would have been saved.

The Division left a wooden memorial in the wood which was replaced by a permanent one after the war.

Chapter Six
October 1916 – September 1917

'The Salient' Ypres (Ieper)

The ancient town of Ypres and the last vestige of Belgian soil that we occupied, was sacred to the British army and to the British people. Not only that, it was one of the key positions between the enemy and the Channel ports, therefore it was to be held at all costs. The Germans had tried once in the June of the previous year to break through, using gas for the first time. The Canadian Corps foiled this after desperate fighting, and at the cost of 8,000 casualties.

On the 16th October the 47th Division had taken over from the Australians, a front of 2,300 yards. On this occasion they caused a good deal of complaint, having left the trenches in the gumboots which should have been handed to us. It was also said they took blankets into the line.

This was depressing country, almost dead flat, intersected by becks, damaged canals, hedgerows and pollarded willows and in winter it became a huge cesspool. Our new Divisional front south of Ypres extended from Bluff Sector at the Comines Canal to the Zwartelen Spur, Hill 60, near Comines Railway. Between Hill 60 and the Bluff was the ravine sub sector and from there to Hill 60 it was partly trench and partly breastwork just below the crest.

The Divisional front had remained static for 15 months and was to remain so for a further 8 months until the battle of Messines. Ready for that, a very large mine had been dug right under the hill. To guard this 'treasure' involved two systems of underground defences. Infantry were responsible for the high level and the surface, and the tunnellers for the low level. If anything should necessitate the premature explosion of the big mine at short notice, a special local operation, involving the capture of Hill 60 and adjoining sectors, was ready to be carried out. Further to the left the ground sloped down to a swamp, There, a continuous line was impossible, so a series of posts, approached only at night across the open, took its place. Contact was maintained with the Division to our left by night patrols.

At the Bluff, where the canal cut through a low ridge, were two spoil banks and the length of these were tunnelled, furnished with wire bunks and lit by electricity, where part of the garrison was in occupation. Adjacent were a cluster of mine craters, these craters were connected by tunnels and there were posts in each.

Near Hill 60, a bridge crossed the railway cutting, connecting the front lines, the parapets were gone. The front line hereabouts was named Marshall Walk.

Immediately behind Marshall Walk was King Street and here one could emerge at night through a trap into a post from the company tunnel below, where the tunnelers were quartered. It was quite spacious and was part of the underground defences of the big mine. I was at this post once from where I had a good view of the vicinity. I was able to see a heavy machine gun firing through a hole in wet sand bags. I remember this tunnel well as the main entrance was in the cutting on the track which gradually rose to the level of the bridge. I was once on some mission with L/Cpl Norcott to the front line. There were some German mortar bombs (minnies) landing in the cutting and one happened to fall unpleasantly close. The blast blew Harry and me down the entrance.

It was a mid October when I rejoined the battalion in the Bluff Sector. I had spent the night in the Bluff tunnel and was making my way up to the 'Wynde', a communication trench. It was already daylight and when I arrived in the front line I was amazed to find no one on lookout, so I went along the trench calling the garrison out, as they were lying in the shelters. They all appeared to be strangers to me. One of the first I saw was a Sergeant, which added to my amazement as to their behaviour. I soon learnt they were new drafts, chiefly 'Royal West Surrey's', and they were in the front line for the first time.

I took one up on the fire-step with me and was giving him some instruction when suddenly there was an explosion, a violent tremor, and we were showered with earth and stones. It came from our immediate right. My companion looked at me in astonishment. That, I told him was a mine and we were very lucky. We were moved quickly to the right where there was a cluster of mine craters connected one to another by tunnels. They had blown a mine between two craters and we were positioned in case the enemy made an assault. A small party of them did cross the 50yds from their trench with a machine gun, but they were seen by some Australians who fired on them causing them some casualties.

I later had to crossed this crater often. It was deep and consisted of fine shifting sand which made it a very risky journey, especially at night. The rain brought loose earth down the sloping sides into the water lying at the bottom. One slip and one would sink into the mud and drown.

Until June 1917, it was to be the same dreary, daily routine. The front lines were so close together, one could hear, when the weather was frosty and dry, the Germans opposite, stamping their feet on the duckboards.

The amunnition dumps were on this road and 'carrying parties' had to negotiate the duckboard track to the trenches. In wet weather the carriers would find it very difficult to prevent themselves slipping on the muddy boards. Some materials were transported by a light tramway. I had the experience of sitting on the platform (that's all it was), which had four small wheels and was about a foot above the ground, and this was pulled by a mule without a rein. We were warned though to watch if the truck gathered any speed as it would strike the mule pulling it. It was quite a pleasant ways to deliver the goods, but snipers were ever present, so one needed to be cautious as there were many places where one could be observed passing along a trench. There was one latrine to the rear of the front line which was avoided wherever possible. It was considered to be a fixed target and only safe to visit in a crouched position, even at night.

Daily the enemy would 'strafe' in the late afternoon for about an hour in the vicinity of Hill 60, and sometimes he would send over his 'minnies' mortar and 'rum jars'. Our 'Stokes' mortars would reply. In some cases there would be, from one side or other, a signal flare for artillery support, in which case the poor infantry would have further cause for blasphemy.

In winter, life in the trenches was purgatory, water to the knees, even, in spite of gumboots, feet suffered. A L/Cpl we called 'QC Socks' collected our wet socks and dealt out dried pairs. The wet ones were taken to a shelter somewhere to the rear of the line, where they were heat dried. Even so, there were large numbers of soldiers who got 'trench feet'. It was no joke walking along a trench with duckboards floating knee high. One lifts a leg, presses the duckboard down to earth, climbs on, and walks towards the other end, with the board rising behind you. The water drained from 'no man's land' as it sloped down to us. Even when the water subsided it was very difficult to clear out trenches.

The winter of 1916/1917 was severe. It often drizzled for several days and nights and in parts there was no shelter. The water ran off our steel helmets and down our necks, which meant carrying parties in greatcoats and ground sheets quickly caused one to over-heat. The body heat inspired the lice to greater activity. Between the shoulders seemed to be the favourite with them, and what a pleasant relief to rub ones back against a sandbag.

Christmas came and our brigade was in the line. The other two brigades were in huts and ate all the turkeys. When it was our turn we had to be satisfied with pork.

It was a white Christmas with deep snow, which thankfully kept the artillery quiet.

During this period there was a gradual return of the less seriously wounded, many of who had spent sufficient time in active service, and had helped to build up our battalions tradition. One afternoon a meeting was held in a hut, and the 'Hounds' of 10 Platoon was born with the object of preserving the 'espirit de corps' of the 'Old Boys'. Our Sergeants thought it great fun, we later included our Platoon Commander, a young 19 year old, Lieutenant Wildsmith. He was a great sport, who enjoyed our company in preference to that of his fellow officers, who disapproved of his playing football with us, and loaning us his gramophone and records. Once, when we were out at rest, he had orders to take us somewhere and give us rifle drill, but no, he led us somewhere off the road, out of sight, and out came a pack of cigarettes to pass round. He was killed at the battle of Messines in June.

We were now wearing the new 'box respirator', instead of the almost useless PH helmet. The enemy had produced a new terror weapon, an improved 'whizz-bang' of greater velocity. No one liked the 'whizz-bang', there was little time to take avoiding action, but the new addition (177mm) went bang-bang with no interval. One could be dead without warning.

I was on some mission from the line in the direction of Ypres. I was following a track which led to a large circular pit about 4 feet deep with a duckboard track all round the inside and small dugouts with entrances about 3 feet high and 2 feet or less wide. I went down some steps and was halfway to the other side when I heard a gun fire, I felt in no doubt it was coming straight for me and I dived into the nearest dugout entrance, my water bottle and haversack jammed, fixing me firmly, I knew there was nothing I could do, so I resigned myself to being blasted in, and against the back wall of earth, or being peppered in the rear with red hot iron fragment. The shell plomped into the muddy ground behind me but never exploded. Once again I had survived. That was the only shell and it had picked on me.

The continuous maintenance of the trenches was made more laborious and difficult by the rain and snow. The earth near the Bluff was like porridge and necessitated revetting (supporting of the trench wall) by means of 'A' frames and expanded metal. The 'A' frames were wooden and when fixed were like an inverted 'A', which had flat instead of pointed bottoms to rest on the trench floor and the cross bar took the duckboards, raising them above the water level. A direct hit would create the heart breaking task of clearing earth, mixed with splintered wood and bent and twisted metal, making it necessary to frequently use the hands.

The appalling weather conditions caused the Divisional Commanders to order that troops in the line were to be given either a hot meal or hot drinks every 4 hours. Soup was brought along the trenches in huge thermos containers during the cold nights, often peppery pea soup, which restored the circulation.

With January came the frost. The bread arrived frozen hard, there was little comfort in the line, but, mercifully owing to the lack of depth of the trench system, when relieved troops were able retire to the many hutted camps, where we could sleep in blankets. When we took the high ground in June, it was wondered, why the enemy had spared these camps as much of our rear area was able to be observed.

February came with temperatures down to zero; I must have been run down at the time as I developed an abscess in the top gum which pushed out my top lip making me look like an ape. When we went on parade our officer asked what the matter was. He told me I couldn't stay outdoors like that, but must go back into the hut and lie down. I must have been asleep when I heard my name called. Our platoon Sergeant wanted me. 'You're on next' he said, and I remembered I had entered the company boxing competition. I was fighting a young fellow from Croydon, I forget his name. I was only too well aware that if he hit me once in the face it would be agonising. I had sparred with bigger and older men than my opponent, and had learnt how to defend myself. I was strictly on the defensive for the first 2 rounds, allowing him to use up his energy, and in the final round I chased him round the ring and finished unharmed.

It is interesting to recall how we came by the gloves. We were coming out of the line for rest, marching along the road when we spotted a figure waiting for us. An American, who resembled a Canadian Mountie in his splendid dark blue tunic, riding breeches, knee high boots and wide brimmed hat. He looked a fine big fellow as he 'fell in' at the front of our platoon saying, 'I guess I am a Tommy now'. Now you know, he should not have said that, because Sergeant Fred Peart replied sharply, 'you are only three years too late mate' which dismissed our American friend. I feel sorry for him now, as he was a member of an advance party for the Americans, something akin to the YMCA I think, who brought gifts of sporting gear like a football and 'boxing gloves'.

The day came when we began practising 'over the tapes' and we knew we were shortly going into action. I was still only 19 and entering my second year of warfare, but I felt different, older and most confident. About this time I was the oldest serving member in my platoon. Truly one of the old boys.

I had got to know most of the new chaps in my company, and had found some lively company among our bombers. There were 3 London Irish lads, Corporal Augustus Smythe, (Gus) an extrovert, Jim Miley, who would often sing 'the wearing of the green 'with such emotion that tears flowed. I had the pleasure of saving his life. Pat Hallett, a right 'harum-scarum', who always looked as if he'd been dragged through a hedge, but a very lovely character and there was Bill Holland, (Holly) a cheerful cockney. Life was fun with them.

One night I was with my pal Lance Corporal Harry Norcott when the gas alarm sounded. We were in an isolated post, so if anything developed we would have to fight it out alone. We were expecting a gas attack, and strange as it seems now, I remember we solemnly shook hands and said goodbye in case we didn't survive. Harry and I were bosom friends and had joined at the same time.

It was nearing the 20th February when we learnt of the plan of a battalion raid on the ravine sub-sector in daylight. The objective, inflicting casualties, capturing and destroying war material (dugouts, machine gun, minenwerfers emplacements, and mineshaft and gas cylinders), gaining information in regard to the front system and destroying a light gun which had been located not far from the German third line. Zero hour was 5pm with withdrawal an hour later at dusk to provide cover. Troops employed were to be the 4 companies of the 'Cast Iron Sixth' with 6 Lewis guns, 1 officer and 20 Sappers of the 520th Company of Royal Engineer, 1 officer and 4 other ranks of 2nd Australian Tunnelling Company, making a total of 25 officers and 640 other ranks.

With the object of deceiving the enemy, there was to be a dummy raid by the 22nd London (Queens) to our left at Hill 60, a small mine was to be detonated in no mans land 5 minutes before zero and a second 2 minutes before zero. The detonating of the first mine was to be followed by a barrage of field guns and 2 inch trench mortars, lifting at zero to form a box barrage in the rear of the craters until zero plus 10 minutes. Trench junctions and strong points behind the enemy line were to be bombarded by Howitzers and 2 inch trench mortars, with smoke bombs to be fired in the Hill 60 area and coloured rockets to be fired behind our lines. Other coloured rockets collected in the Bluff craters to our right, were to be fired in salvo's of 6, 9 and 12 minutes after zero, while the 41st Division artillery were to keep high ground south near the canal, under heavy fire throughout.

The 20th February came and we went up and relieved the battalion on the front to be raided. At last, the thought of action instead of being sitting targets. We were going to pay 'Jerry' for the trouble he gave us all winter! Everyone was confident and in high spirits. I remember the details of this success so well. I wrote home a few days after the event stating 'much has happened during the eleven months in the 'Salient', there is much I can relate. The letter gave an accurate account of this raid as we were so well versed in every detail, and as things went as planned it was not difficult to record it. Totally disregarding all penalties, I sent it by green envelope, which somehow, and fortunately, escaped censorship.

When the second mine exploded, the 2 minute hurricane bombardment commenced. I was in my jumping off position with number 10 Platoon in the front line on the right flank of the operation. A communication trench entered the bay I was in, the trenches here were chiefly breastwork. The parados were very sketchy with many open spaces where one could walk through without having to climb on top; also the communication trench mentioned was non-existent for several yards before the line. It was due to this that I escaped being 'blotted out'. We could see the shells and mortars throwing wood and earth from the enemy front line. I stepped several yards back into the open space behind our position from where I had a better view. The overhead fire from the heavy machine guns sounded wonderful, a continual swish. Then, tragedy occurred. I plainly saw the heavy trench mortar bomb drop short and fell plomp into the bay I had just left, killing 5, amongst them my dear young friend Tommy Fleming, to whom I had but a moment ago been talking". I had no time to dwell on this as the barrage lifted and we were away. There was little resistance as the enemy was taken by surprise as they took the dummy raid as the real thing.

I was with my old friend Corporal Harry Norcott, and jumping into the front trench we saw 2 Germans laid out on the ground. Thinking of taking them prisoner, we tried to raise them, but finding them severely wounded we left them. I had a large canvas bag full of grenades for our bombing section, as they were to clear the communication trench to form a flank. The support lines were severely damaged and yielded a considerable haul of prisoners, amongst them, the officer in command of the sector. The troops, who went on to the third line, killed and wounded a large number of the enemy as they attempted to escape to the rear. Our lads had a field day, destroying everything to hand. They found no gas cylinders, nor was the light gun found. Enemy dugouts, machine gun emplacements were wrecked by the mobile charges thrown into them. This nearly caused us severe casualties as during the noise and confusion the Royal Engineers had great difficulty in diverting the triumphant raiders away from nearby dugouts containing a fizzling charge of guncotton.

The results, 1 officer and 117 other ranks captured, a large number of enemy killed, 2 heavy and 3 light machine guns destroyed, large quantities of documents, maps and papers found and a great deal of destruction in the enemy trenches. Our costs, 11 ranks killed, 2 missing, 4 officers and 59 other ranks wounded, with 3 of these dying of their wounds.

We held our line until relief after dark, and marched back to the huts. Approaching the huts my old pal Sergeant Albain who had been held back with many others, was waiting to greet us. He searched the ranks as we entered the camp and espying me came forwards and embraced me. He was evidently loath to lose me.

The Battalion had won 1 - Distinguished Service Order, 4 - Distinguished Conduct Medal's, and 16 - Military Medal's in the record raid on 20th February.

About the end of March the 18th London Irish was selected to repeat the raid of the 6th London, but on this occasion the enemy was better prepared. They brought up Storm Troopers in close support and their artillery preparations were more complete. The London Irish were shelled on their way up to the line. When they went over the top the enemy put down a 'nutcracker 'barrage on both front lines and brought up their reserves. The result was a pitched battle in the enemy reserve line with heavy casualties on both sides. The continued barrage forced the raiders to deviate to both flanks.

Before this raid commenced, I had been on a working party and returning tired and weary through lack of sleep, I sat at the entrance of the dugout built above ground from where I could see the gas shells exploding round the artillery batteries near the road. Then silence. Being so fatigued I began to doze, when suddenly from behind the enemy a single heavy gun fired. Instinctively, I was on my feet, and went immediately into the front line. In no time the company had manned the parapets but were prevented from observing as a machine gun opposite was traversing the front line. As it swished to and fro, it sprayed us with earth. At the end of our company front, I selected a bomb bay and frantically began preparing for repelling the attack I expected. The enemies trench was little more than 30 yards away. I laid out some grenades on a board in readiness and to my dismay I saw that the pins were rusted in, so I quickly eased them after closing the bifurcations with my teeth. A chap named Dell had joined me, but he wasn't eager to look out, so it was up to me. I was not going to be taken by surprise.

Waiting for the machine gun bullets to pass, I backed out of the bay into the trench and stood on tiptoe. There opposite was a daring German with a machine gun mounted on the parapet, exposing himself to his waist. I realise his job was to keep all enemy heads down and so he had to be put down. I ran round the traverse into the next bay and told Corporal Norcott what I had seen. We decided it was a job for a sniper, so he sent along for McCarthy. Being about St.Patricks' Day, I remember the little green flag with a harp, attached to his rifle; he took a quick look and prepared for execution. As I heard the shot, I popped up in time to see the German topple back into his trench, leaving us free to observe the front line. By this time it was obvious by the racket going on to our left that the raid was in that direction. The London Irish only took 18 prisoners and lost 160 ranks.

The day after this, the Divisional front was reorganized and the 23rd Division took over Hill 60 sub-sector. Hardly had the newcomers settled in, when the enemy opened heavy artillery and mortar bombardment on that sector and at 7pm began a raid. They penetrated the higher level of the underground defences (the high and low defences protected a huge mine). There followed a confused struggle with Infantry and the diggers, the Australian tunnellers taking part. However, little damage was done, one bomb thrown into the empty Company headquarters and another into the area of the dynamo supplying electric light for the tunnelers. The 7th London took over the spoil bank sub-sector on the other side of the canal. Little did we know at this stage, it was in preparation for the battle of Messines in June.

It would be very hard for someone to imagine the battlefield in which we fought unless they had actually seen it. It was just one vast stretch of pulverised, poisoned earth and mud. The effect on you was worse than shelling or fighting, although that had to be endured as well. Willpower alone kept you going, if you lost this, you were finished.

The names of villages in Flanders did not seem to have the same romantic sound as those we knew in France. They seemed to match the landscape, Zillebeke, Verbrandebmolen, Kruistraat, Dammstraase, Hollebeke, Elverdinghe, Vooremazeele, Bossingle, Steebvoorde, Vlamertinghe, Ouderdom, and Reninghelst. They were near the trenches, where there were very few civilians who had stayed. Here and there, such as at Dickebusche, where some cottages remained undamaged, the women made a fair living after we had been paid. It would be café, pomme de terre frites and deux oeuf (coffee, eggs and chips) . There was no life here.

There never seemed to be a dull moment on the line, the trenches were so close, and minor raids and fighting patrols so frequent. When they occurred, and it was feared that we were about to be overrun, up went the flares signalling for artillery support, which, when it arrived brought retaliation fire from the enemy. So if you thought the night was quiet and the opportunity arose for a little doze, death could come without warning. I got into the habit of convincing myself I was going to get out alive.

I remember another funny moment, it was one dark night when we passed another work party, 'are you the West Riding' someone asked, and one of our wags replied 'no, we are the bloody Sixth London walking'

It was soon after the big raid that the King came out to visit the Salient and we were promptly honoured, because of our success, by providing his guard of honour during his stay at Cassel. The guard was in the charge of a sergeant from the Guards, who seeing one of our lads fidgeting, shouted 'what are you doing', to which the lad replied, 'chattay sergeant'. The look of horror and disbelief on the sergeant's face, and the tone of his voice, as he exclaimed loudly 'chattay', lost him all respect, and he was relegated to the bottom of the scale. He showed his ignorance as he should have known that we carried our lice with us always, they were indestructible.

Sometime later George V went up near the trenches, some clever people let him go by car. As we found out later the roads were under observation from the high ground held by the enemy and I saw the very narrow escape he had. I was on the corner of the crossroads at Reninghelst, we had been told to line the route. From were I stood I could see in two directions. The road from the line entered a dip below me and I could see this road plainly for perhaps a mile until it disappeared over the horizon. I saw the car come into view followed by a shell burst on the road. There followed a salvo of four 5.9's shells at a regular distance all on the road, just missing the royal car each time. I don't know how many witnessed these dramatic few seconds as I have never heard it referred to, nor have I read of the incident.

We began to receive some of the later call up of 'Derby' men, which included married men. (Derby men were so named after Lord Derby, director general of recruitment. He encouraged men to voluntarily register their names and be called up if it became necessary. **KBM**). There were two older fellows who joined our Platoon, they were old enough to be my father, and so out of place in this hell on earth. It sadden me, especially, as they attached themselves to me in the trenches, preventing me being with my particular friends. Once when we were being strafed by mine werfer mortars bombs, I was watching them carefully, as the bombs wobbled and woofed in our direction, they never seemed to take their eyes off me. They were such innocents; everyone loved them, Johnson and Lunn, like twins. I could have given them the slip as we entered the trenches, but I had not the heart. 'Young Merry' they christened me. I am not ashamed to say, I am near tears when I think of them as they were killed at the Battle of Messines.

When in later years my friend Norcott and I inspected the Menin Gate War Memorial, we found the names of Johnson and Lunn, and we shed some tears.

I am purposely trying to avoid mentioning the horrors, aptly described in many books in many libraries, and which were all too common to those on active service. I believe we developed a defence against nausea and the sights we witnessed, otherwise how could we have remained sane. speaking for myself, I realized that death and wounds were part of the horrible experience and were expected. I saw, but pretended not to see, dismissing it from my mind immediately. I could pass a corpse which had lay a few days with horrible disgusting bluebottles crawling in and out of the mouth and nose, and swarming round the sightless eyes. It did not do to dwell on these things, as they were all too frequent.

I became friendly with a newcomer by the name of Ted Villa (though I am certain now, he was Eduardo). He was a small swarthy customer with a strong Mexican accent and little fear of death. He was well liked but was unfortunately killed in the battle for Messines Ridge. Some 40 years later, when old comrades met, our Company Quartermaster surprised us when Ted cropped up in the conversation, 'did you know who he was ?' he asked us, and went on to say he was the son of Pancho Villa, the famous Mexican revolutionary leader of about 1910. It had been a secret, and so he had to administer an allowance on his behalf.

One morning on turning out for 1st parade, we met a new young officer who soon proclaimed he was a cricket fanatic. Without loss of time he had a 'C' company team and challenged the transport to a match, to be played for a sack of figs. Our company won and when we retired for the night the figs were opened, only to be found rotten. There ensued a battle royal, figs flying in all directions. It was useless our Sergeant MP opening the hut door, shouting 'leets out'! He tried it twice, to be met with a hurricane of figs, so gave up.

One night in the front line I was on the fire step, on lookout, when a strange thing happened to me. It was a beautiful moonlit night. I was watching thin trails of cloud passing over the moon's face, giving it the appearance of moving swiftly across the sky. I was engrossed, trying to imagine what there was beyond that moon in the infinite space beyond, when I seemed to leave my body and look down upon it and thinking, if I were to be hit I would not feel it. It could have lasted but a few seconds. I never spoke of it and thought no more of it until, some years ago someone in Oxford, I believe, had a letter published in the 'Radio Times' asking anyone who had experienced such a thing to write to him as he was evidently making a study of this phenomenon (I have forgotten the name he gave it) I wish now I had answered him to find out more.

Owing to the nature of the ground near Hill 60 which made it impossible to occupy, it was necessary to man the isolated posts, which needed extra vigilance and silence. One night I and 2 others were in a sap (a trench to conceal the approach to a fortified place) near our frontline where a 'double block' had been made. Jerry occupied one side of the block and we the other. As it began to get daylight, I was on watch for the last hour, my back was to the enemy and I had a mirror fixed to my bayonet so that I could observe without being seen. Suddenly in the mirror a face appeared, I froze, thinking if I can see him, he must see me. He was a scruffy, unshaven specimen, he was so near his face filled the mirror. He was looking towards our front line and surely must have been unaware of our proximity. I didn't rouse my companions in case they precipitated a disturbance. It was possible this was the post where my friend 'Miley' lifted an empty sandbag, found a hole, and put his eye to it, and was greeted with 'good morning Tommy'.

The Canadian and Australian tunnelers had their rations brought at dusk and we were sent as a carrying party, to take them up to the railway cutting. On one occasion the Canadians unloading, gave us a whole cheese, which just goes to show how superior were their rations.

On another occasion, this time for the 'Aussies', the same thing happened. I happen to be the last back after delivering my load, when my dream of back to huts was dashed; I saw one of our party standing besides a crate of 'bully beef'. It was his first time up and had for some reason convinced the Sergeant in charge that he was unable to manage it, so I was expected to go back again. It was useless to argue, as the others had disappeared by then. I was extremely angry, and said that if I was to go up again, this blighter was coming with me. I hated carrying these crates, especially up to the cutting, as for most of the way up the railway tracks was twisted. There were duckboards laid on the sleepers and many of the slats were missing, making it very dangerous in the dark. I made the fellow walk in front of me, while I got angrier, as the corner of the crate cut into my shoulder.

After delivery, we turned about for the return journey, making the cause of my suffering walk behind this time. It was getting dark very quickly and I thought of getting out of the cutting quickly, but I had by now to tread carefully. My companion was all for speed and tried to gee me up, but I soon let him know that had he got me up there, and he would get to safety as I wished. Suddenly the Whiz Bangs began a strafe. It was in enfilade fire, as the shells were flying low over the cutting, almost parallel to the front line. Now I had one of my stubborn fits, as my friend behind began tried to get in front of me, and I decided to teach him a lesson, so I deliberately slowed down. I could understand him getting nervous as the shells were bursting too near for comfort. To hurry invited a broken leg. The more frantic my friend's efforts to get ahead, the slower became the pace. I was fully aware I was gambling with my life, but I was getting some wicked enjoyment from it. However it all ended well. I felt sorry for the victim later, and rather embarrassed at the respect he showed me adding that he thought I had no nerves.

We had a pair in our Company whose antics caused much amusement. Hobbs ('Hobbo') was a clodhopper from Watford to whom some innocent had given a stripe. He had a booming voice over which he had no control, and which was a positive danger if he was within hearing distance of the enemy. His perpetual enemy was the diminutive Harvey, who had a very pink complexion. Hobbs, who was 6ft. tall and 'Titch' Harvey, would have made a good music hall turn.

The slower thinking Hobbs would irritate Titch, and he would berate Hobbs violently, getting pinker and pinker. Added to this, little Titch could never get a small enough pair of gumboots to fit him. However, because this pair happened to be with us when digging the assembly trench for the forthcoming battle, it ended in tragedy.

It was a dark night, and the enemy was rather nervous, which meant that he was sending up too many Verry lights. We were digging just in front of the support trench with the wire behind us. Hobbs who unfortunately had promoted himself to 'ganger' (a foreman of a gang of workers), and therefore considered he hadn't to work, only to boss everyone, which got him nowhere. He was being told to 'shush' which only made his voice increase in volume. Then Titch Harvey lost his head and began lambasting Hobbs with his tongue, which immediately switched on the enemy machine guns. Before we could take cover the bullets were ricocheting off the wire making a queer noise and making sparks. Maitland-Allison who was near me, fell. We managed to get him down into the nearby communication trench, to find that a bullet had entered his abdomen and came out of the rear. He died before we could get a stretcher. He wore a declaration ribbon which puzzled even the high ranking officers. It was a 'Delhi Durbah' Medal, the only one I ever heard of, the medal was issued to commemorate King George V's Coronation Durbar celebrations in British India. Hobbs came in for much strong criticism and insult, but, he was so thick, he had the hide of an elephant.

I had another experience of this sort when Hobbs was in charge of a party pushing a load of pit props up on the light railway to the bluff. The end of the line was behind the support trench, and we had to be careful on the bends in case the wheels screeched, in fact the operation had to be carried out in silence. We arrived, and Hobbs had to boom out instructions which were totally unnecessary. Despite requests to keep his voice down, the need for which he refused to acknowledge, he brought whiz bang fire on us. Some got beneath the loaded wagons, others, including myself made a dash for the nearby entrance to the tunnel in the embankment. Harvey spitting venom all the way got one foot stuck in the mud which drew off his gumboot.

During May things began to move and we soon realized that something big was coming off. Dumps of ammunition began to multiply. Stores of all sorts and guns of all calibres slowly accumulated.

We were taken from the line for intensive training over tapes, which represented the trenches we were to capture. The preparation for the Battle of Messines seemed perfect in every detail. Maps were studied by all ranks near to the time of action. I, along with a friend in my platoon, was asked to help copy these maps. My friend, because he was an engraver, and I, because of my reputation for drawing funny cartoons and sticking them up in the trenches. I sent a pile of them home to my girlfriend who kept them when we 'called it a day' which I now regret. I would have liked to have kept them myself.

CHAPTER SEVEN
7TH JUNE 1917

The Battle of Messines

By the middle of May things were hotting up. There was much activity just behind the lines, which could be observed by the enemy from Messine ridge, and when our artillery increased activity, so the enemy retaliated. On our side there was little cover, in consequence our artillery suffered. So did transport, with a heavy toll of horses, which troubled all the horse lovers.

An Army order came and ordered that all troops should convert trousers into shorts without cutting them. They had to be turned from the bottoms up inside the leg and secured and pressed. You may think this proved a serious problem, but I can assure you the result was perfect. I remember going into an estaminet in Reninghelst, where two old biddies got familiar whilst examining my shorts, and had to be warned off.

On the 13th May we left Reninghelst, marching via Boeschepe to Abeele. The next day we continued through Steinvoorde to Ebblinighem, just to the east of St. Omer and on the 15th arrived in Acquuin, a total distance of 40 miles.

Here the battalion continued to train for the forthcoming battle until, on the 31st May it marched to St.Omer, boarded the train to Poperinge and finally marching to Ouderdom.

It would seem that much had been learnt from the capture of Vimy Ridge by the Canadians, where thousands of aerial photographs had been shown to all ranks, and each battalion objective was explained in great detail. This information, said Julian Byng, was more important to the troops taking part, than if it fell into enemy hands. So with us the troops knew well in advance what they had to do, the date of the attack was the only secret.

To give assistance to the French, who had suffered heavily in an attack from the Aisne, our battle was hurriedly pushed forward. The 47th Division (London) was to attack astride the Ypres–Comines canal, which meant handing over the Hill 60 sector to the 23rd Division who were on our left.

The 10th Corps (23rd Division, 47th Division and 41st Division) was to capture 6,000 yards of fronts to a depth of 1,500 yards, including the heavily trenched position 'the Damstrasse' which was on the right, the White Chateau (which was now a heap of rubble), both banks of the canal and Battle Wood on the left. Of the 47th Division, the 140th Brigade attacked from the right of the canal and the 142 Brigade to the left of it. This was to be part of the 2nd army offensive on a 19 mile front, with an artillery preparation in which over 2,300 guns were employed, throwing 90,000 tons of ammunition.

On the 5th June full of confidence and in good spirit our battalion the Cast Iron 6th paraded in fighting order and left Ouderdom advancing across country by platoons at 50 yard intervals to Ecluse Trench (ecluse is French for a canal lock) which as the name implies was alongside the canal by the large damaged lock gates.

These last few hours before the battle are the testing time. I remember the behaviour of those round me, for the most part they were sitting silent, deep in thought, and there seemed to be little sign of nerves. When the time came for synchronizing our luminous watches, I got to my feet and looked to the rear. I remember peering into the dark trying to see a ruined farm house, until our artillery fire of unprecedented volume burst into action. Now the farm house appeared in a silhouette against the brilliant flashes of artillery. Turning to the front I saw the dull glare of the exploding of 22 mines, the earth shook like never before. On the right of the canal, the 7th London (Shiny Seventh) and 8th (Post Office

Rifles) assaulted the first objectives, including the White Chateau. At 5.30am we the 6th, filed out of the old French trench to take a position by the old front line.

In his speech to us before the battle, General Lord Plumer said he wanted to see no prisoners, what a hope! we didn't kill prisoners. So as I advanced up the communication trench to the second assembly, the parapet was crowded with seated Germans. Waving to them, I shouted 'good morning Jerry' as I went forwards over the old front line. I saw one poor fellow buried to his waist, his face was like raw meat, and the skin seemed to have been blasted off.

Each company had been given compass bearings, so no difficulty was encountered in keeping direction. On reaching the White Chateau, we found the 7th had failed to capture it, and the enemy prevented further advance. Machine guns from the Chateau grounds enfiladed us, the 6th and 15th (Civil Service Rifles).

The 6th had a difficult task to execute once the Chateau was secured. It had to take the ground to the left, and get into a position to advance with the creeping barrage. At the Chateau the 7th were digging in. Here we were halted and told that a two minute hurricane bombardment would fall on the Chateau. I was with our Platoon officer, Mr Wildsmith (19 years old), Johnson, Lunn and Lance Corporal Manning. They all took shelter in a large shell hole, which was on the extreme right of the Chateau. A little to my left I saw Company Sergeant Major 'Chic'Bitten run up the heap of rubble from where he saw two enemy machine guns firing from positions below. He threw two bombs which scattered the gun crews, and having no more bombs, continued attacking by throwing bricks. I ran forwards to join him, by the time I got there he was on his way down and the barrage was just starting.

When the barrage ceased, I returned to the shell hole to find my platoon comrades gone. The shell hole had had another shell burst into it, I am pretty certain it was one of our own. (I should imagine that this happen many times during the war, friendly fire, as we call it these days. **KBM**). Mr Wildsmiths' head was blown off, his tunic collar was still smouldering, poor old Johnny and Lunn were dead and Lance Corporal Manning was missing.

After the war I saw a photo of Manning in a daily paper operating a switchboard in a hotel, he had been partially blinded.

Again, it seemed my curiosity had saved me. I hurried on passing some stables and the outhouses where there were many dead Germans. As I was threading my way though the barbed wire to find my Platoon again, a German artillery officer and a gunner came out of the woods and asked me how to get through. Noticing the officer's pockets were bulging with maps and documents, I was quick to relieve him of them.

I was soon back with my Platoon again and Sergeant 'Flo' or it might have been Sergeant Fred Peart commented that they thought I had gone home. They little knew how nearly true it was. (I am confused about the fact that my Grandfather was in the 6th City of London Rifles, yet at this time his platoon officer, Lt.Wildsmith was in the London Cyclist Battalion ? I can only assume that officers were moved between battalions as the need demanded. **KBM)**

Part of our advance had surrounded a second set of stables, where we captured two enemy offices and six men. We now entered in a clearing between the woods, and advanced walking within 30yds of our barrage, up a slight slope, passing a deserted enemy pillbox. We reached the top of the hill, which was our objective, without further resistance. Here we commenced digging in and laying out coils of barbed wire.

From here we saw the Germans retiring in disorder towards Hollebeke. One of our platoon members was sent across towards another wood to find where the enemy were. He got no more than halfway before he was fired upon. The enemy could not have seen us, for we would have been sitting targets, as we had yet insufficient cover.

During the night I passed several times through an earthwork of a machine gun post, walking over a hump in the ground, which in the morning I saw was a German corpse almost completely buried. Several times during the night the steady bombardment increased as suspected counter attacks were dealt with. The whole operation was superbly prepared. All objectives were secured on the first day and casualties were mercifully light. The 47th Division suffered 21 offices killed, 76 wounded and 1 missing. Other ranks, 359 killed, 1764 wounded, 82 missing. Of these the 6th London suffered, 2 officers and 30 other ranks killed and 81 wounded. A miraculous result, due to five months infinite preparation and overwhelming superiority of artillery. At a single blow we had taken out part of the ridge, which was strongly entrenched, and had been occupied by the Germans since the latter part 1914. Our troops were able to keep within 30yds of a wonderfully accurate creeping barrage. During the 24 hours from the beginning of the attack one 18-pounder battery of our Division fired 6000 rounds.

We were involved in several more raids to straighten the line, before being relieved on the 10th June. We rested in Ecluse trench, before the Battalion moved out of the line on the 15th to Ontario camp. We then marched to Caestre, and on to Ebblingham, near Hazebrouck, where we remained for 12 days in barns and outhouses, training and reorganizing.

Here a funny incident happened. A few of us were returning after an evening in the town. As we crossed the field to our barn, we stopped to watch the milkmaid milk a cow. At that moment Lance Corporal French appeared, he had been drinking, which always made him aggressive. He began to annoy the young lady, who directed a spray of milk into his face; it took all of us to keep him off of her.

It was very hot and at Blaringham we took to the cool waters of the Canal Neuf Fosse. On the tenth day here we went to the Divisional aquatic sports where there were entertainments. I think the best was the last event, the odd craft race. I believe the canal here was as wide as the Thames at Hampton Court. The launches passed up the canal and we thought we had seen the last, when all eyes turned in the direction of a tiny vessel chugging along, trying, or so it seemed, to catch up with those gone before. On its side was painted 'shit or bust'. Up went to a tremendous roar of laughter and applause as it continued it hopeless course. It was an absolute 'hit'.

On the 28th June we were on our way back to the trenches, and I remember well at our first stop on the way, some of us spent the afternoon in a pool organising swimming races amongst ourselves.

The next day we moved up to Ridge Wood, resting the night in bivouacs, and on the following night we moved into the front line. Here we patrolled, with occasional small scale raiding.

We took our turn in support, which meant taking rations and supplies to those in the front line. At dusk we would line up in 2 parties, the one in front took the rations. We had to take care we were not seen, as about this time in the evenings enemy 'spotter planes' were very active. To avoid surprise we never went the same way 2 nights running.

One evening whilst waiting for the Sergeant in charge to lead us off, a shell passed over the heads of the leading party, which I was in, and sadly killed the last two men in the second party. We had to wait for quite a long while for our Sergeant who was involved in capturing a German strong post. The nights were very short at this time of year, so it was breaking day when he returned and we entered the wood on our way back to the old German front line, where we were in residence. Suddenly the German artillery began searching the wood with their new high velocity 'whiz bangers'. All hands scattered to the right and jumped into the communication trench and high tailed it for home.

On our way back a chap called Jim Miley was making heavy weather of it, so I slowed down as we went round the traverses, but he still wasn't keeping up with me. I could hear his feet plomping through the several inches of water in the trench. I was anxious to push on as the shells came uncomfortably near. I was also annoyed because the rest were well on the way home, leaving us well behind. When I was about to leave one bay, I waited to hear his splashing feet in the bay I had just left, but I heard nothing. Fearing he had been wounded, I dashed back, but he was not in the previous bay. I found him in the bay before that one, unconscious, sitting down in the water. Jim was never to know of his good fortune. There was no sign of injury. I managed to get him his feet and put his arm around my neck. He began to moan, but never opened his eyes. How I managed to drag him along the trench, I will never know. When at last I found a spot where a shell had blown in the side of the trench, I was able to drag Miley up the slope and out. It was easier going on the top and I soon piled him into his dugout without disturbing anyone, as the fellows of the carrying parties were fast asleep. I have never told what happened.

The next day I realised what was wrong with Miley. I remembered a day when some of my platoon, for some dark reason, volunteered to hump the company rations up to the front line in the 'Oppy-Gavrel' sector in Arras. When we arrived at the Company Headquarters, we found Jim Miley semi conscious. It was obvious what had happened as he had been carrying the rum jar. In spite of vigorous shaking and face slapping, he couldn't be revived, so he was quickly piled into a dugout and a blanket pulled over the entrance, which was very fortunate as the Commanding Officer came pass a few moments later. It was this incident which convinced me that during our rest, on the way up with the rations to the old German strong point, he must have found the rum jar and over indulged himself.

During this spell in Oppy-Gavrel, we happened to be repairing the trench. I was standing on top watching salvos of 5.9's dropping between us and the heap of the White Chateau, when suddenly, a friend named Cooper collapsed in a fearful state. I was alone with him on the post. He seemed strange, was silent and in a state of shock. I noticed a peculiar smell about him (I found this again later when handling shell shocked cases amongst the German wounded). On reporting to Sergeant Flo, he asked for volunteer to carrying him to the White Chateau, where the forward dressing station was in its cellars. I volunteered.

So giving Cooper a fireman's lift, I made my way quickly cross the line of fire, just after each gun had fired. Having managed that without fault we entered the Chateau stairway down to the cellars. Here I left him to be treated.

In August the 58th London Division arrived on the Ypres front and many friends were met once more. As the 58th only reached France in January 1917, many drafts from a 2nd Battalion had joined the 1st Battalion. Raids were taking place all along the Ypres front which indicated another offensive. Haig wanted to liberate Belgium, and on July 31st the offensive commenced, which was the overture to Paschendael. Haig was determined to pursue this offensive, despite warnings against it.

After a successful raid on Oblique trench we were relieved and moved in small parties to Curragh camp for a fortnight. On July 12th the Sussex relieved us and we marched back to Westoutre and from there on to St.Omar by train arriving on 15th.

Here we began training for another attack and on the 24th we were moved by bus to Poperinghe.

CHAPTER EIGHT
DIVISIONAL POLICE - JULY 1917

In Poperinghe I was informed that I would be loaned to the Divisional Police for traffic control duty. I am of the opinion that I was chosen to give me a well earned break. I had been in action for 18 months and my leave long overdue. I hadn't seen home since Christmas 1915. This was a stroke of good fortune, as although I wouldn't be entirely out of danger, it would mean regular hours, better rations, regular sleep and was able to view the war from a different angle.

Arriving at Divisional Police Headquarters, I was assigned to traffic control and issued with an arm band. Little did I suspect how uncontrollable the traffic was, although we had a great deal of authority, it was sometimes impossible to impose.

One of my first turns of duty was at one side of the town square with my partner on the opposite side of the square. There were two roads in and two roads out and we had to regulate the traffic to keep a steady flow. Daylight was fading and there was a heavy flow of traffic, all in a hurry to get up to the line and back, lorries, limbers and general supply wagons. The Australians were the worst; they would create havoc, as they had no respect for authority. We had to do what we could in an impossible situation. So it was left to another fellow a little way up the road, where there was a junction. His job was to keep transport from double banking, what hopes! It seemed a free for all. Drivers whipping up their teams to get ahead, if they could. They would have triple banked had there been room. The poor chap at this post could do nothing.

In daytime there was less traffic, and a chance to stop someone if need be. Take the water cart; the orders were it was forbidden to ride on the shaft, one comes along and the person in charge was seated on the shaft, so he is stopped. He puts on an air of innocence, then gets off and walks besides it, until he rounded the corner.

The worst incident I had was with an aggressive 'Aussie' returning with his horse and limber from the line. He came down the road towards the Menin Gate. Instead of going on through Ypres, he wanted to cross outside the ramparts to the Lille road. There was a corduroy track laid for that purpose, but on this particular night part of it had been put out of action, and I had been posted to warn drivers not to use it. All was going well until the Aussie came up, and it was 'get outer my way you!' 'I told him he could not get through, but he whipped up his horse and slashed with his whip at me, with that I drew my bayonet and threatened him. I knew that was it a lost cause and comforted myself by thinking of the difficulties in front him, he was going to get well bogged down.

Come to think of it, I had a far worst incident on that Menin road, when I wished I had my rifle with me, as you never carried a rifle on this duty. On this occasion I was posted at night at the Birr crossroads near Hooge on the Menin road. (When visiting Ieper I always stay in a charming little hotel called Kasteelhof t'Hooge, it is on the site of the stables of the old Hooge Chateau. **KBM**) I had a small shelter of ammunition boxes filled with earth. My duty was to stop limbers returning from the line from speeding, as the noise would attract enemy shelling.

When the traffic seemed to finish for the day, I crossed the road and entered an artillery dugout and sat with the gunner, who was seated beside the telephone. Here I remained until daylight when my duty ended.

When daylight arrived I began to make my way back to my dugout which was next to the Menin Gate, suddenly in an enemy plane came over the tree tops from my right. When he spotted me, he descended almost to ground level and opened fire upon me. Along the roadside were trunks of what had once been an avenue of trees. I quickly took cover behind one. I could distinctly see the two aviators in their leather clothing and goggles. The plane turned before reaching the road and made off over the trees. I continued on my way, but to my surprise it returned, so I took evasive action once more as the sound of hissing bullets missed me. 'They've got a cheek' I thought, oh how I wished I had my rifle, I am certain I could have scored a hit.

There wasn't a great deal of excitement in the work, although out duties were varied, most of it was not very important. One was on the roads where the troops headed across country to the trenches; one had to insist that certain intervals were observed in each column, as the enemy were shelling the back areas to the rear of the front line. They often bombed the hutments and sandbags were used round the huts to protect the heads of the sleepers inside. Somehow one felt much safer doing these duties, than being in the trenches. Can you imagine the Menen road at night, pouring with rain, mud, with a mass of transport using it and the enemy shelling, trying to prevent any horse, wagon or man arriving at their destination? Our job was to try and prevent disorder and unnecessary loss of life.

In the Divisional history it was reported that 'traffic control was most efficient and the Military Police seemed always to be standing at the allotted corners, no matter how hot the shelling was, ready to help with all kinds of information, military or otherwise'.

On the 30th August the Division was transferred to the Oppy-Gavrelle front, relieving the Royal Naval Division which included the 28th London Regiment (the Artists Rifles). I was still assigned to the police and our accommodation was in the cellars in the Saint Catherine quarter of Arras. We had not much to do on this front. The battle and capture of Vimy Ridge by the Canadians in May had pushed the enemy down into the Dourai plain, where our line was a series of well defended localities, with strong posts from half to three quarters of a mile apart. These were garrisoned Companies and the gaps between were covered by artillery and machine guns.

In the rear of the line and looking down on the village of Bailleul, was the ridge through which, in a cutting, ran a road from where the whole plain was under observation. Here we had a post and the objective was to warn all comers that the moment they entered the cutting, they could be seen by the enemy. Hidden by the steep slope we had a hut, with a table and benches outside. Lorry and general supply wagons came in for scrutiny, as for some reason drivers weren't supposed to give anyone a lift, not even when they were empty. Some clever person issued us with notebooks, and ordered us to stop every vehicle which carried a passenger, taking the drivers name and number. What a fiasco that turned out to be, all day long we were taking names. They were handed in and we heard no more of it. Was the A.P.M. responsible? If so, it was all right for him, he went about on horseback. I am glad to say the name recording stopped after a couple of days, the poor old foot slogging infantry deserved the ease they could get.

Whilst on this job, I realized that all these people behind the line depended on the thin line of watchers on the firestep, doing their one up and two down all night, making it possible for those behind to get safe nights sleep. Just outside Ecurie one could see the old front lines from which the Canadians had left in a snowstorm and took the ridge in a well conceived and executed plan.

One afternoon I went to the canteen, where I bought a tin of 50 Players cigarettes, returning, I stopped to watch a gang from the Chinese labour Corps, some were carrying earth in something suspended from a pole. When two came near I offered them a cigarette, immediately, the rest stopped their chanting, dropped their loads, and ran to me. Needless to say my cigarettes vanished. The Chinese looked a motley crew as they marched away after their work, their clothing was of all descriptions, bowler hats, trilby's and caps. (about 100,000 Chinese were in the Chinese labour Corps, although they were not employed as fighting men, some 2,000 died, many as a result of the Spanish flu. **KBM**)

During this period there was a discharge of 710 gas projectors into Oppy village at a time the enemy division opposite were being relieved, followed by a raid by the 17th London (Poplar and Stepney Rifles) among others and further gas projections.

The chief event was a combined raid over a 1000yard frontage to a depth of 500yards on the Arras – Garrelle road by companies of the 23rd and 24th London (Queens). The success was mainly due to the continuous Lewis guns firing on the gaps in the wire made by our artillery.

This raid began at 4.30pm. The excellence of our artillery barrage was so accurate that our men had trouble initially get at the fleeing enemy. Within five minutes the front line was carried, the enemy were overwhelmed; hundreds of the enemy were killed, with few prisoners being taken. Besides enormous damage inflicted, 9 dugouts were destroyed, with some set on fire, and in some the occupants refused to come out. One man killed nine of the enemy single handed and one officer five. There was a reason for so few prisoners: shortly before the raid, enemy planes dropped bombs on the London, killing relatives of some of the men. A notice board was left in the raided area saying 'we'll teach you to bomb London'.

Soon the Divisions were to be relieved and moved to the Cambrai front and I was returned to my battalion. My journey up to the line with my Company was a day that I could not possibly forget. Three lucky escapes from death in one afternoon.

I had noticed that the dugouts in the loamy soil had not been properly revetted and in some places had collapsed. Arriving in a support trench, which was very deep, we were allotted our dugouts. I was given one some 4 feet high up the side of the trench with room for only one person to jump up and crawl in. There was no room to sit up so I threw in my pack and rifle in first. Before getting in I remembered a friend had had a parcel of magazines that morning, so I thought I would borrow one, lie down and rest after the long march up. By this time everyone was probably dozing, as blankets were down covering the dugout entrances. A short chat with my friend and back I went with something to read, but during my absence the earth above my dugout had collapsed burying my rifle and pack. I would have been buried alive.

My pack and rifle recovered, I was escorted to the front line where I joined my old friend Lance Corporal Harry Norcott. We were to share a newly constructed dugout made for two. It was of the steel cupola type, mounted on two courses of sandbags. In went my pack and rifle again as the afternoon strafe began with artillery and trench mortar. To my surprise we were withdrawn to the safety of a large, deep, newly built dugout, leaving a few men on lookout (an innovation this).

Soon the strafe ended and we returned to find the entrance to our dugout blocked by earth. Harry and I found two shovels and began removing the earth. During this I heard the pop of a mineweffer and watched the mortar bomb shoot up and overhead. When it began its wobbly descent it was obvious we were in danger, we dived to the ground and the horrible thing hit the earth a few feet from us. We looked up at each other in astonishment, we could not believe it, it had failed to explode.

After some more digging we entered our dugout, I looked at my pack which I had left behind. It was where my head would have been resting. Stuck into it was a piece of shell shrapnel similar to a spearhead, some 10 inches long. It had gone through my writing pad and pierced an unopened tin of unsweetened milk. How lucky can one get?

A few days later I was on my way home, which I hadn't seen since Christmas 1915. Home to what seemed a strange land, where people had no idea of the conditions at the front. It was useless to talk of it, as folk looked at you in disbelief, and believe it or not, we were somehow happy to return to our friends at the front.

I returned from leave in time to march to the Cambrai front.

Chapter Nine
Battle Of Cambrai And Into
Captivity November 1917

On the Cambrai front on the 29th November we took up positions in the Hindenburgh Line (a German defensive position running from Arras to Laffaux) which had been captured on the 20th. A few hours later we moved forward with difficulty in the dark to the support line of C Company from a sunken road to the left of Bourlon Woods. The battalion orders were to hold this key position in the Salient.

The enemy attack began at 8.30am on the 30th November. There had been no time to dig trenches to link up with the battalion to our left. It was obvious the enemy were trying to isolate the 6th Battalion, who were being attacked on each flank; a desperate situation was becoming worse. At around 2pm, the Company to our left was under attack on three sides. Our artillery support was inadequate and enemy planes were making low level attacks on us.

During the battle C Company was moved to the left, to help the company on the left. During this move my platoon was occupying a shallow trench, about 3 feet deep, at the bottom of a slight slope, which prevented enemy observation. I was lying on top of the parados, looking through a pair of binoculars I had picked up. I could see no movement in front of us. As we were moving position, I saw two of our company come under fire in a trench not too far away, they looked isolated and in a confused state. I asked the officer in command if I could go to help them. I waited for a lull in the firing, and then made a dash to them. Whilst they rested I agreed to take the watch. So for one hour I sat on the parados, as there was little room in the trench for three of us.

During this time there seemed an apparent lull in the attack, so I decided to move forward a little way to find some shelter where I could rest, I was very tired, having not slept since the night of the 28th. I found a dugout in a trench mortar position, which was in excellent condition, with steps from the entrance. Here I met Lance Corporal Elijah French. I suggested that we should not enter more than three or four steps in case of a booby trap. So we found a cigarette and shared it.

It wasn't long before the silence was broken by violent machine gun fire; there was no artillery fire, so were not suspecting immediate danger. We then heard the voices and I said to Elijah 'they are not our chaps', but before we could move out, we found ourselves looking into the barrels of eight rifles.

Why they didn't shoot or throw grenades down the entrance, I don't know. I took the initiative, saying to Elijah, in a defiant manner 'we are not raising our hands' and we climbed out of the pit. I began to speak to them in English and French. They were very young and friendly, and a few replied in French, so we continued chatting. How ludicrous it seems now, while the attack was in progress, there was I, hands in pockets, finding out their ages and how they had been enjoying peaceful conditions up till now.(The enemy had pulled troops back from the Russian front, where fighting had ceased). We soon parted company as our chaps were firing rapidly from behind us. I often wonder what became of those young Germans, as there seemed to be no one in command of them.

We moved forwards and crossing our front line it was plain to see how we had suffered, all along the trench our dead were lying. We crossed 'no man's land' to a road, where we came across another wave of the enemy lying in wait for the order to advance. Three of them pointed their rifles at us, alas we were caught !!!!

We were escorted to an officer who was gathering prisoners. As prisoners arrived he was sending them in pairs to where the enemy wounded were lying. Each pair was given a pole with a ground sheet suspended, this became a makeshift stretcher and we were to pick up their wounded and carry them. My partner was our Sergeant Sleet and we were directed to one wounded German who was above average weight, and we were ordered to pick him up and march.

We eventually dumped our load in a large hollow behind enemy lines. Here a German doctor was attending to the wounded on a table. We proceeded further back behind their lines and I found myself with four enemy stretcher bearers and we began chatting. They found it very uncomfortable carrying the stretchers on their shoulders whilst wearing steel helmets so I collected and carried them.

I was happy enough at this stage, no one seemed to find me out of place, no one seemed to really care and I had not the faintest idea where I was going.

We were passing an artillery battery in the furze where a huge chap came out and wanted the ring I was wearing. He wasn't demanding, but I thought it safer to offer him an English coin I had brought back from leave. He went off perfectly satisfied.

We came to a sunken road where the four Germans with their stretchers made for the door of an estaminet. As they did so a German officer came out. Seeing me, he demanded in an angry voice as to what I was doing there. 'Off with you' I assume he must have said, strange I thought, nobody wants me. There were two doorways to the estaminet, one to the bar and the other marked 'keller' (cellar). As the officer disappeared inside with the four bearers, I slipped quickly down to the cellar, having no idea what to do. Down in the cellar sat Jerrys in full kit. I went across to the furthest side and sat on an empty chair. They showed no surprise and were friendly; the chap next to me gave me a drink of 'schnapps', which they all seem to carry in their water bottle. They were soon on the move however, and I went out with them.

As I stood on the bank of the road I could see some Germans escorting a party of prisoners, at the front was our Captain Cannon, I was ordered to I join them.

We stopped for the night in a small village and were put into the loft of a barn. During the night the planes bombed the area and scattered some of the roof tiles. In the morning we were made to double round the courtyard threatened by an Alsatian dog if we slacked.

Soon were on the move again, arriving in a barbed wire compound in a field, where there were two ruined cottages with the upper floor gone. It was amazing to see names and regiments written on the walls, with remarks such as 'roll on the big ship' and 'send on Blighty'. This time I had plenty of company as we were gathered with more prisoners.

The next day as we were marched off I noticed one of the guards looked like an Englishman. He was tall, athletic, spoke good English and was very pleasant. What made him look English, was the fact he was wearing 'puttees'.

When we stopped in the afternoon for a break in a village, some of the inhabitants noticed most of us were hatless, so they kindly sorted out some headgear and handed them out. But one nasty little Jerry began snatching the hats off, throwing them to the ground. The pleasant chap in puttees, evidently in charge, made him pick them all up and hand them back. We stayed here for the night in another barn and had our first food since capture. The villagers boiled a large quantity of potatoes in their skins for us to eat; this is all we had, nothing else, which filled us with wind in large quantities.

We eventually arrived at the railway at Le Quesnoy and on arrival were herded into the square to join a few thousand more prisoners, who were being photographed and interrogated, all this being viewed from the balconies by our ecstatic enemy. For the first time I felt humiliated and very angry, and made my first mistake which almost brought me trouble, but taught me to use cunning in the future.

The interrogating officer was approaching me along our ranks; I was in the second rank. He stopped and asked the fellow next to me where were the 25th London's, this was the Cyclists Battalion. I hadn't the faintest idea where they could be. I feared the chap next to me might tell, I nudged him to stop him saying. Unfortunately the officer spotted me and asked why I had nudged him. Before I had time to answer he said 'we know more than you do, you know' All my damaged pride came into operation and I fairly exploded. 'I expect you damn well do' I blasted, which was something he hadn't expected. In a threatening voice he said 'would you like to spend a few days in cellar with bread and water only'. He passed on. I impressed those around me, but they were so concerned that, as we marched away, I was made a walk on the inside, where I wasn't so easily seen.

We were taken to a church, which had a thick layer of straw on the floor, and soon after the same interrogating officer entered with two men. Those who were anxious for me buried me beneath the straw until he had left. 'He was looking for you' they said.

The next day we boarded a train for Germany. It was an awful night, one I will never forget. As we approached Germany we ran into heavy snow, we were in cattle trucks and could only see by standing on tiptoe and looking through a narrow slit. It was bitterly cold and no one had an overcoat. We could only crouch together for warmth.

As we passed slowly through one station, some hateful person tried to throw snowballs into the wagons. We knew we had arrived in Germany for someone spotted Aachen West as we passed through a station. Arriving at Dulmen in Westphalia, the doors were slid opened and we jumped out of the wagons landing up to the waist in snow, we were herded by the guards to the platform to be counted.

CHAPTER TEN
KRIEGSGEFAN GENELAGER, DULMEN

The outlook the next morning was very bleak. The camp appeared to be in the middle of a clearing in a forest of pine trees. With the snow it was bitterly cold which kept everyone inside. At the first opportunity the guards started to relieve us of any belongings we had. I had a fountain pen which I did not wish to part with. As I approached the desk, I observed what was happening, so I secretly slipped the pen into my sock and managed to get away with it.

We were in large huts, with a huge stove in the centre. At this stage we had our sergeants and corporals with us. Our chief concern was with food, the fish they gave us for dinner was unfit for human consumption. It was delivered in a tub and was the colour of smoked haddock; it reeked of ammonia and was so salty that no one could eat it, in spite of being ravenous. When the sergeant in charge of the hut saw it was not going to be eaten he refused to serve anymore and it was removed.

We were offered some peculiar food; I remember some strange black, hard dry lumps of meat, which caused much speculation as to it origin. Another strange food we were given looked like fine yellow sand in sweet water, we never discovered the ingredients of this mysterious mixture which was appropriately named 'Sandsturm'. It was impossible to eat, one spoonful was quickly ejected. So we were left with three alternatives, boiled cabbage, an anaemic substance which looked and tasted like water that fish had been boiled in and two slices of black, sour, soggy bread. It was no wonder that there was an endless to and fro to the latrine buckets.

The other puzzle was our drink, ersatz coffee, was it made of acorns or chestnuts or chicory. It was rather bitter, so my guess was chicory as it was grown in plenty on the continent. We never at any time had any sugar or milk. The pangs of hunger were constantly felt and the talk of food became obsessional.

The habitual drinkers and smokers had an additional problem. There was no tobacco or beer. Our guards were little better off, one went to great pains to show me and explain to me what he was obliged to smoke. He showed me a bagful of chopped leaves, amongst which were some that looked like oak. It had the same smell as herb tobacco. I remember an attempt at smoking it, but quickly stopped.

We weren't to remain long in the 'Fatherland'; we were soon transferred to Tournai in Belgium, where we hoped conditions were going to change for the better. This was wishful thinking. Here our Non Commissioned Offices were moved to another location. We were left in the care of sadistic, old and unfit for combat guards, who did as they pleased with us without hindrance.

CHAPTER ELEVEN
THE WORST DAYS AS A PRISONER - TOURNAI, BELGIUM
1918

I remember leaving Dulmen Camp in January 1918 on a train load of POWs, proceeding leisurely up the Meuse valley heading for Tournai. On boarding the train we were handed Red Cross emergency parcels. As I searched my parcel for a snack I came across a small piece of wrapped cheese that closely resembled a piece of soap, a commodity for which Jerry would trade his eyeballs. I had this idea and intended to risk a fiddle.

Our train soon pulled up at Namur station. I looked up and down the platform for a likely victim. As one came near, I gave him, in my best spiv manner, the old 'pst, pst!' When I had his attention, I cautiously revealed a glimpse of the bait and whispered seif, soap, 'he couldn't believe his eyes. A quick bargain for cigarettes, a furtive glance to the left and right and off sneaked my victim, leaving me praying for the train to move on. The train was shortly underway and knowing it was now safe to do so we enjoyed the joke to the full puffing on our ill-gotten fags, while imagining our victims face as he tried to wash with a piece of cheese.

We eventually arrived at the cavalry barracks at Tournai, there were no comforts or privileges here. We had seen no Red Cross parcels since Christmas. (These parcels were sent via Holland and

Switzerland by organizations at home). We had no one in authority to protest at the lack of nourishment or the ill treatment by the 'posterns' (guards) as our Officers and NCOs were imprisoned elsewhere. Our only means of communication was through a fellow prisoner, a Jew from Liverpool who spoke German. Our uniforms had been confiscated and replaced with work clothes. Head wear was German forage caps which had our number stamped on a metal plate at the front, in place of our flannel shirts and woollen vests we were adorned with thin exotic cotton shirts. Those who had no boots were given wooden sabots, as socks wore out we were given pieces of cloth to wrap our feet in. We had been issued with unbleached pillow slips, these we cut three holes in and wore them as vests.

Our daily routine was early breakfast of ersatz coffee, nothing else, no milk, sugar or proper bread. We were then marched to work, sometimes up to 6 or 7km away, the furthest we named 'the long trail'. We returned at about 5pm for the only meal of the day, a bowl of soup (cabbage water, potato meal, occasionally a few bits of horseflesh if it was available from the nearby knackers yard), one very moist, brown sour loaf of bread, if you can call it that, divided between five of us, never fat of any sort and nothing sweet, except Sundays when we got a spoonful of marmalade or jam and a spoonful of very soft white cheese containing caraway seeds. It was crazy to attempt saving a mouthful of bread for the morning as even if one slept on it, it would be gone by morning.

We had been given an enamel bowl which was an all purpose utensil. A piece of wire was thrust through a hole upon which was threaded our identity disc, and we could then hang the bowl from our belts. From the bowl, we drank, ate and washed in it. We got no soap, but were expected to wash our clothes thoroughly each week, for on Sundays the Commandant inspected them. Each item was shown separately, each piece held out by holding each top corner, a hard rap on the knuckles was customary if someone's wash was not up to the standard required.

It was not long before we were in a pitiful state; it was surprising we were able to work at all. Each day it was common for some unfortunate person to be assisted on the return journey from work, having collapsed.

I remember one early morning parade, most of the guards were still finishing their breakfast and we were outside, lined up and waiting to be counted. By the wall was a dust bin where, soon, some of the guards came out and emptied out their mess tins, a disturbance soon breaks out in the ranks with a stampede towards the bin. The fighting and mauling was pitiful to behold and disgusted me. This reminded me when in Germany, a friend and I had crawled under the wire fences into the cookhouse compound and raked the midden for potato peelings, which we then washed and boiled so at least they were clean. The risk was thrilling.

Soon, unfortunately, it was my turn to be taken ill at work. This was at a cement works which we were preparing to house ammunition. I realized I was going to have difficulty getting back to our quarters. Strangely, one of our guards seeing my distress, stayed with me to help me back whilst the rest of the party went on a head. I cannot remember which one it was, but I liked to have thought it was Schmidt. He, I remember was the only one of a few with any humanity, a mild and amiable person. I had never come across anything like this before, 'Smithy' walked beside me allowing me to take my time, several times I had to stop to rest and he would wait patiently. Passing through a village he knocked at a door and took me inside and asked someone fetch a doctor, who gave me a bottle of medicine.

I was then taken to a German medical room, where the unsympathetic person on duty took away my medicine and asked me to supply him with a sample of urine. I was alert enough to realise what he was looking for, blood, a sign of dysentery. I do not remember a lot of what happened, it was like a dream, I was taken upstairs and put to bed. During the night I must have been delirious, I remember someone bringing me some food, but I have no knowledge of eating it. I am not sure how long I lay there, I cannot recall being given any medicine, although I stirred once and vaguely remember seeing a German doctor.

I finally came too and found myself on a paliasse (straw mattress), fully dressed and inside my trousers, like an enormous napkin, I was wrapped in a sheet. What a state it was in, full of excrement. I managed to make my way downstairs and somehow cleaned myself up.

Eventually I returned to the work camp where I saw Schmidt talking to another guard we called 'Froggy' because he looked French with his goatee beard; he was pointing to me and smiling. He was the exception and I remember him with some affection, for I am convinced that during that time I was so bad I could have died and no one would have bothered.

Some short time after we found ourselves being hired out in small parties, which led to slightly better food. We had new uniforms that had arrived from England, life seemed a little more bearable.

One of the first jobs we had was levelling land for an airfield. Two enormous hangers were erected; these housed the big Gotha bombers which the ground crew told us with delight, were for bombing London, but we got an opportunity to taunt them when we heard one had not returned. There was an attempt to get us to load the bombs, but this soon stopped when they found detonators had been removed. We were replaced by Russians.

One morning on the way out to work we passed through tiny village, where some women offered us mangel wurzels (type of root vegetable). The senior guard, who was a right anglophobe, started ranting and raving and ordered some of the guards to chase them. I saw one woman get her hand caught in her door where upon one of the beastly guards hit the hand with his rifle butt.

Another major task that came our way was to lay a full gauge railway. We were moved to a convent in Froyennes, where part of the building was being used as a hospital. The railway line was to be a branch from the main line near Tournai to the hospital, which was to receive the casualties from their offensive. We removed soil, laid sleepers, carried railway track and laid prefabricated points. It was a painful task given our condition.

Nearer the main line an embankment was necessary and soil had to be raised. When the rails were fixed in place we had the monotonous task of packing the sleepers tight with ballast. This was done with picks which had a square end for packing the sleepers, it was a lengthy task. When the wounded arrived we had to carry them from the train on stretchers, we then had the difficult job of getting the stretchers up a spiral staircase. The care shown by my fellow prisoners when dealing with the enemy wounded was a direct contrast to the brutal treatment we had experienced from some of our guards. Upstairs, the nuns went about their nursing duties regardless of nationality.

While the railway was in the making we were made to dig a trench near the convent wall which would act as air raid cover. We learned afterwards that the enemy had bombed hospitals at some of our bases, Etaples being one of them, so it's possible that retaliation was expected. Whilst digging the trench, a British plane flew in a low circle over the convent, the German guards fled for their lives to the accompaniment of howls of derision from their laughing charges. The next morning another plane flew over and dropped a bomb in the yard, killing a few chickens, which our lads, in the absence of the frightened guards, collected and manage to smuggle back to our quarters.

Harvest time arrived and the local farmers needed help in the field, so work parties were dispatched. I went in a party of 30 prisoners, which had two guards and a cook. We marched to a tiny village call Anvaing which was on the outskirts of Renaix (the centre of the cotton industry). It was here I met a good friend called Arthur Baines who came from Bolton.

We were billeted in the school, which was one large room fitted out with double bunks. Just outside the village was a large sugar factory and in the grounds were cement canals where the sugar beet was washed. At that time in the canals and surrounding area were many large tree trunks waiting for transportation, some of these trunks were

3 feet in diameter; the problem was how to get them onto railway wagons. The smaller ones were rolled by using wooden levers, the larger trunks had to be moved using a 'gill'. The 'gill', as my northern friend told me, was a contraption used by tree fellers to cart tree trunks. The idea was to raise the tree with hook and chain and using weight of men as counter balance. On one occasion, owing to my co-workers fearing an accident was about to happen, they released the hook and chain and leapt from the shaft without warning which almost ripped me open from bottom to top. The huge hook shot up like a missile from a catapult. This caught the bottom of my trousers and ripped the seam right up to the top, how narrowly I missed disembowelment.

Another dangerous job, where many could have been injured was when we were at a branch line that ran into the 'sucrerie' (sugar factory) where there was a loading platform. One morning on this platform we found two large boilers, each were mounted on four wheels, with a single shaft for two horses. These we had to move down a ramp to ground level so that a farmer could take them away. As we were to discover, we should have had some experienced person directing the operation, for as soon as the boilers began descending down the ramp the iron wheels in the front twisted and turned, taking the shaft with them, which lashed from side to side uncontrollably, throwing some of the lads aside, the rest fled to a safe distance.

It was about this time that our circumstances altered in our favour, partly due to better relationships between prisoners and guards. The cook, who was a pleasant chap, managed to give us better food and we had a delivery of parcels from the 'Red Cross'.

This was the second occasion they had arrived, where the others went, I have a good idea, for in Germany the people were also going hungry. Also our uniforms (provided by our regiments) arrived. There were black with 2 inches of khaki down the outside of each leg, a 4 inch band round the left arm and a band around our peaked caps.

Clad in our new uniforms our confidence rose no end. One could not help feeling superior, when comparing the general appearance of the German army in their thread bare uniforms. The lads felt proud when they marched and began whistling as they went. We began to learn that the Germans were being clobbered. We got a good feeling that the tide was turning.

Whilst at Anvaing I secretly made the acquaintance of a Belgian schoolboy. He regularly sneaked potatoes to me, until he was spotted and threatened by a guard. I took an instant liking to this boy called Louis, and this attachment remained until his recent death. I still correspond with his wife and family. I felt sorry for the Belgians, especially the poor children, who offered us their daily roll, which they received at school. At my request Louis obtained an exercise book from school, on the inside of the cover was a map of Belgium and N.E.France. I had decided, when a favourable occasion presented itself, that I intended to escape.

The time came for all of the working parties to rejoin the working battalion. Soon we were back in France at St.Amand. Our first job was unloading timber from the barges which were on the River Scarpe. Each morning as we marched to our work, we passed a house which had it's french windows open. Inside someone would loudly play on the piano 'Tipperary', through which we would join in singing the words. Our guards went up and down the ranks crying 'cease', but this did little good.

We found the Germans were becoming disenchanted, owing to the bad news they could not help receiving from the front. This became very evident when we were switched to the Army Pioneer Park No.5, which was retreating. Train loads of army stores arrived for us to unload and store undercover. Amongst other things we stacked sandbags in huge piles, which occasionally we could 'accidentally ' drop one on a guard beneath as he was unable to see us. The sandbags told a sad story, we found out that they had been made by civilians in Germany. Any available material seems to have been used, curtains, tablecloths, clothing, all sorts, so telling of the conditions in Germany. We were really in the mood to sabotage items, which we dumped in the nearby river. We soon began to hear gunfire from the front which day by day appeared to be getting closer. The tide was turning.

We were soon on the move again, this time we were to be used as horses, for there were sixteen large farm wagons piled high with kit. Twenty men manned each wagon. The pulling was done in two shifts of ten as the countryside which we were traversing was relatively flat. I began noting names of places we passed through, and checked them on the map given to me by my courageous little friend Louis. On the trek we saw things, dead horses, bomb holes, wrecked tractors, evacuated cottages. Some of these cottages were at Conde in the Valencienne area and the evacuation must have been sudden for there was uneaten food on the table. Personal belongings had obviously been hastily gathered. I picked up a picture postcard from one of the cottages. I am uncertain of the reason for the departure of all the inhabitants, but I suspect they were forcibly removed, possibly for work in Germany. In fact it was not until Pervwelz, near Mons that we saw civilians again. Here we had the luxury of a bath in the brewery, which as far as I can recollect was only the second bath in ten months.

Our next stop was at a convent in Siraule, then on to Soignies where we slept in barns. By this time, from the map, it looked as if we were heading for Bruxelles, where I felt I had a good chance to slip away unobserved. Our hopes ran high as we passed Hals, but was not to be, the nearest we got to the capital was a signpost to Ixelles. Beyond that we joined the road to Kessel-Loo, a suburb of Louvain, which I decided was far enough. All the time our hopes were that by some mysterious way we would join up with our army, which we knew was on the advance. Although I had no set plan, the attraction was to get into Bruxelles first. I knew what failure meant, as I had seen how escapees were treated.

This long trek was pleasant enough, the going was easy and the weather fine and we didn't have to march back and forth to hard labour. Not much happened on the trek, I recall only two incidents, one humorous, the other serious.

In the first instance, as we progressed along the road, an enemy staff car full of top brass, came flying along without any consideration for the lives of 'Englisher Sweinhunds', almost peeling off those of us on the offside, who had to take urgent evasive action. Two German soldiers passing on the opposite side of the road began a heated argument, which we were able to witness as the convoy had halted. One (bless his heart) was furious because of the arrogance and callous disregard for human life, and was making a good job of it, whilst the other took an opposite view and did not care for English pigs. This led to blows which made us laugh and cheer.

The second distraction occurred not too far from the place we were stopping at for the night, although we were not to know that at the time. We were passing a farm and two women came out and began verbally abusing our guards. The one in charge caught one of the women and with the help of his men made the poor soul walk behind the wagons. We finally arrived at our resting place and the battalion formed up for dismissal, with the woman to the rear between two armed guards. 'Battalion dismiss' came the command, no one moved. This surprised the person in command and he had no idea what to do. So we made the most of it and told him 'let the woman go or we don't move'. What a joyous moment, 300 angry voices letting him know were no longer underdogs.

On reaching Kessel-Loo we found new quarters in a school. Around and on top of the walls was barbed wire with bells attached which would ring if the wire was disturbed. It was a fairly large school with many rooms. Some optimistic lads thought to defy the wire, get over the wall and on to the road. Eventually one lad did try, the bells sounded and he found himself unable to get back and so jumped on to the road and ran. We were all assembled in the playground and information was sought as to who was absent, of course none of us were going to provide it. It was cold and dark and we were threatened with being kept standing there all night until someone named the culprit. Next to me was a despicable specimen who suggested we told, so that we could get back into the warm. I told him I would kill him if he dared opened his mouth, which seemed to change his mind.

Sometime later the absentee for some strange reason, walked back through the gate, and was ordered to stand all night in front of the lavatories. There was a screen in front of these and when it was safe I made my way over to it and hid behind. There was only one sentry about and he was someway off. I knew the fellow had no great coat and only plimsolls on his feet. I whispered to him that I would bring all the things he needed and leave them on the seat. He should then get permission to enter the lavatories, put on the articles and hope the sentry would not notice the transformation. It worked.

CHAPTER TWELVE
ESCAPE AND BRUXELLES

Returning from work one day we saw one of our airmen in difficulties, he was descending in small circles, but must have successfully landed as we heard no crash or explosion.

When we returned to our quarters a few dozen of us were removed into a neighbouring house, which had a big back yard surrounded by a high wall. There was a tall wide gate which opened on to the street, and our sentry had the gate open sufficiently to enable him to view the scene outside. We were all gathered in the far corner of the yard; Arthur and I were walking towards the sentry to speak to him. As we reached about halfway, an airman, probably from the plane we saw earlier, was escorted in and put with the others. Immediately he was surrounded by an excited crowd hungering for news. Seeing the excitement, our sentry left his post to investigate. As he had his back to us, I seized the opportunity, telling Arthur to keep close to the wall and follow carefully without haste. We reached the gate and slipped through, boldness it had to be.

Whilst we went through the town it was essential that we had to stroll as though we had every right to be there. On the road as we left the town we met a few limbers containing looted fowl. The leading one was being pulled by a cow and I could not resist taunting the driver. 'Nach Paris' I shouted, for he would definitely never see Paris and I just managed to avoid his whiplash.

Darkness soon engulfed us as we plunged on. There was only one uncertain moment, as we passed an estaminet on the opposite side of the road; the door opened causing a shaft of light to cross the road. We turned our faces away hoping our black uniforms would conceal us. Three Germans came out, watered the hedge opposite, and then went back inside, much to our relief. Apart from this we met neither man nor beast until we reached the outskirts of Bruxelles.

We eventually came upon a building showing a light from inside. Entering warily, we found it to be a dance hall, almost every inch of floor space was filled by civilians sleeping, next to them their bundles of belongings. Arthur and I managed to find a space to lie. We stayed for a short while, but finding floor very uncomfortable, we decided to leave. We needed food and a hiding place, and from whence it would come from we had no idea.

We walked a short distance. Suddenly a man appeared and to our relief and amazment we recognized him, he was from our own regiment and had escaped earlier. He was dressed in a smart suit and was able to walk the streets unconcerned.

On hearing our story, he gave us the name and address of the Belgian lady who would assist us. M'lle Anna Van Dael, Avenue Jean Volders, St Gilles, Bruxelles.

We soon found the premises and were received by a small lady possibly around 60 years old. Miss Van Dael was no ordinary person, she was in fact one of the Belgian heroines. She was one of 'Nurse Edith Cavell's' organisation to help, shelter and assist escapees into Holland. (Edith Cavell was born in 1865 in Norfolk, and was a nurse in Bruxelles when war broke out. She played a key role in running the underground life line for escaped allied prisoners, but was eventually found out by the Germans and shot in 1915. **KBM**). Anna Van Dael had been arrested on suspicion more than once, but released due to lack of evidence. Her home had been searched, but she was always too clever for the enemy. For her courage she was decorated by the French and Belgian governments after the war.

We were hidden in the attic and remained there without incident until the Germans marched away.

I remember the morning after the Germans had left, we were sitting at the table eating breakfast with a wonderful feeling of being free when suddenly the Midi railway terminus opposite erupted. The wagons in the sidings were loaded with shells which the vengeful enemy had time detonated. The explosion shattered windows and shells were flying over the roofs bringing down tiles. I was on my feet immediately. Arthur put his head out of the window for a better view and was nearly struck by shrapnel from a shell that hit the wall a few feet away from him. I made for the landing calling to Arthur to follow. Miss Anna imploring me to descend to the cellar, but seeing I was determined to go outside, she stamped her foot saying 'you phlegmatic Englishmen'.

Arriving outdoors, our attention was attracted by some screaming women and children. Beside the railway was a footpath and several cottages had suffered considerable damage from the explosion, the occupants were in a panic, whichever way they turned, they were in danger of injury from falling tiles, glass and bricks. Ignoring the police, we went across and shouted to them to come out and follow us. They did and with the help of two Scouts, we led them to the safety of the Grande Place.

That afternoon, we had a visit from the Scouts with a message from their parents inviting us to dinner that evening. The evening dinner was splendid.

We were now free to enjoy real freedom, especially as at this time we were not under the jurisdiction of the army, and we were in no hurry to rejoin it. We were given ration cards and money. All cinemas and other entertainment were free. We had a great time. One of the first Bruxelles attractions we were obliged to be taken to see was the famous 'Manikin Pis', a little boy who keeps the fountain basin full. We took a tram ride to the field of Waterloo, viewing the panorama of the battle and climbing the steps up to the Lion, where we left our initials (This is unbelievable, my Grandfather, a vandal. I did actually look for their initials when I visited the Lion in 2007, needless to say they were not there.**KBM**)

The VICTORY parade through Bruxelles was a memorable sight. Many allies were represented, Belgian, French, Algerian, British and Americans. Each had their bands, mounted troops, infantry and artillery paraded. We stood in front of a group of British Officers, who asked us who we were, as they had never seen our uniforms before, they expressed surprise, but beyond that they seemed uninterested.

Back at Miss Anna's house a young French soldier, who had been hidden elsewhere by Miss Anna had come to collect his medal and papers that she had kept for him. She removed a 4" x 4" tile from the fire surround and drew them from the cavity, the Germans had not discovered her secret hiding place.

Miss Anna had told us on several occasion, how she longed to taste white bread again, and one day I learnt that rations were available in the square, so I went along and obtained a large loaf. She gratefully accepted my gift. We had learned a lot concerning the dangerous work she had undertaken during the war, not from her lips, but from those who had worked underground.

Soon transport would become available for our repatriation, but not before we had seen the twice life size statue, in plaster, of Edith Cavell erected in the street (this was replaced with a permanent one later) and the newspaper 'Le Libre' on sale openly. It was claimed the German commandant of Bruxelles found a copy everyday on his desk.

Our day of departure came and it was a very emotional occasion. Here I had emerged from boyhood to manhood, having been tried and tested to the utmost. I was sorry to leave Belgium and the heroic people I had known. Our train left for Calais and on the way we had the opportunity to see some of the picturesque parts of the country, such as Gent and Bruges. Hugging the coast we crossed the old front line near Dunkerque and arrived in Calais. We were herded on to a ship and in no time the coast of France was out of sight and we saw the cliffs of Dover.

On landing we were transported to Dover Castle and I was struck by the sound of English being spoken again after nearly a year of guttural German, rural French and Walloon. We were given a printed message of welcome from the Mayor and citizens of Dover.

The return home was far from the happy homecoming I had expected, there was a change, and one heard from all sides complaints of shortages. There was that lack of communication I had noticed when I was on leave, there seemed little understanding of the horrible conditions endured by the troops.

On arrival in London there was a month's leave and I had become no.322103 of the City of London Rifles again. At the end of my leave I was sent to Sevenoaks and the Royal Defence Corps for a short time.

I soon found myself bound for Denham Lodge near Uxbridge to guard German prisoners. There weren't many, I used to take a small party on the tram to work on a local farm and leave them. They were a happy lot and had little to complain about. Their rations were far better than we had received, and the folks on the farm would give them meat pies. Now you would expect those of us who had suffered brutality and malnutrition to have shown some resentment, giving them a taste of what we had endured, but I'm happy to say I never saw this happen. We even played football with them. I must however confess to dealing out a small amount of justice to their interpreter, Jaeger, who was an arrogant young Prussian N.C.O., who because of his status took liberties. He would enter our room, which had formerly been a large lounge and now had ten trestle beds on each side, without invitation and make himself too familiar, until one day, no doubt taking his country's defeat too seriously, he began throwing his weight about to the extent that he annoyed some who were resting on the beds. He began excusing the sinking of the Lusitania, saying it was carrying ammunition (Lusitania was a quadruple screw steam liner and was sunk by U boat in May 1915 off the coast of Ireland with a loss of over 1000 civilians). Our angry response caused him to get more arrogant and he declared he didn't have to work, and no one would make him. I could not stand any more; I reached up to his high silver braided collar and shook him, telling him very plainly, that I would make him! Without warning he swung his right arm up catching me a fair whack in the eye, which blinded me for a moment, when I could see again, I went after him with murder in my heart. He had fled to his room upstairs. I went back downstairs and waited behind our room door. A short while went by and the door slowly opened and he poked his head in, where upon I grabbed him by the tunic and pulled him inside. I then went berserk, hitting him left and right about his face again and again, causing him to back into the corner and curl up. There were at least six Sergeants lying down on their bunks and not one of them uttered a word, despite the knowledge that striking a prisoner was a court martial offence.

When I calmed down I went to see how much damage I had inflicted on Jaeger. The sight of his face caused me some concern, both eyes were black and his mouth had been bleeding, so I went to the cook and obtained a generous portion of raw meat which I applied to his face. Fortunately, when we paraded for pay the following morning he was out of sight. Our Officer asked what had happened to my eye, to which I replied 'I knocked it Sir'.

I had not finished with Jaeger. He was a means of financial gain to me, and aided me to get home at weekends. I would buy tins of 50 cigarettes and bottles of beer and sell them to Jaeger at a profit. Jaeger was humbled. I thought he had been punished enough, and I forgave him as it was not in my nature to bear malice.

In April I received notice to attend at Crystal Palace for the purpose of demobilization.

CHAPTER THIRTEEN
TIME WITH THE BRITISH
LEGION 1927 – 1939

With the 1914 to 1918 Great War over, I was full of confidence after my experiences over the 3 years spent overseas, but I missed the life and comradeship. The next 2 years were full of frustration for me. I found myself jobless and in poor shape. I began to work with my father when he started up business again. Although not happy, it was a turn for the better.

In 1927 I met a chap called Charles Harris, I learned that he was the Surrey County Standard Bearer for the British Legion. He invited me to come along and join in.

This was a period of rapid expansion for the Legion. Branches were being formed in towns and villages and they all had to acquire a Standard and on these occasions there had to be a dedication service. My friend 'Smiler' Beal and I went everywhere with the Wimbledon branch Standard in support of the Surrey Council of British Legion. We, along with Chas Harris soon became well known in the county and I began to enjoy life again, being active amongst men who valued comradeship as I did.

I was one of the Guard of Honour at the station when the body of Earl Haig was put upon the train bound for Scotland and again when Princess Mary opened the new wing of the Nelson hospital, Merton.

In time we raised sufficient funds to purchase a large house, 'the Lookout', in Kingston road, Merton for our H.Q. and club. The opening ceremony was performed by Sir Joseph Hood, our M.P.

I ended up holding a number of posts which quite often involved me most evenings of the week. Executive committee member, deputy standard bearer, games committee member, secretary of children's and Christmas outings, secretary entertainments committee, assistant publicity officer, indoor games captain.

Indoor games competitions were held at British Legion clubs all over Surrey, which included anything from snooker to chess. Big county rallies were held at Ranmore Common, Dorking and at Reigate Heath. The children's outings took place in the summer. They began in the countryside, but were soon transferred to the seaside. As many as 350 travelled by train from Wimbledon to Littlehampton. We hired the funfair for an hour and then went to the local British Legion Club for lunch. In the afternoon they were taken on a motorboat to Arundel and back. The children had a wonderful time.

I went for the first five years with our Standard to the 'Festival of Remembrance' at the Albert Hall. The first year in 1927 was followed by a torchlight procession to the Cenotaph.

When the Second World War came I was drafted in to the National Fire Service to serve my country again.

At the end of the war I attended a service at St. Sepulchres and met up with so many of my old Company. We all keep in touch by correspondence, which help us to be well represented at important occasions.

Sad to say, in 1975 our number is now only about five, but the memories of my departed comrades stay with me.

James Bass

James was born in 1897 at the family home 'Millers Mead' in Colliers Wood, Merton, SW London. It is still there today, but no longer owned by the family

**Family portrait about 1908 –
William, BARTON (Father), James, Violet,
HANNAH (Mother), Stanley**

James Bass. Builder. 1827 - 1911.
Wife Mary Ann Legge
Children - James: Louisa: Barton Alfred: Sydney.

James's Grand Father 1908

Haydons Road School about 1906 James Bass

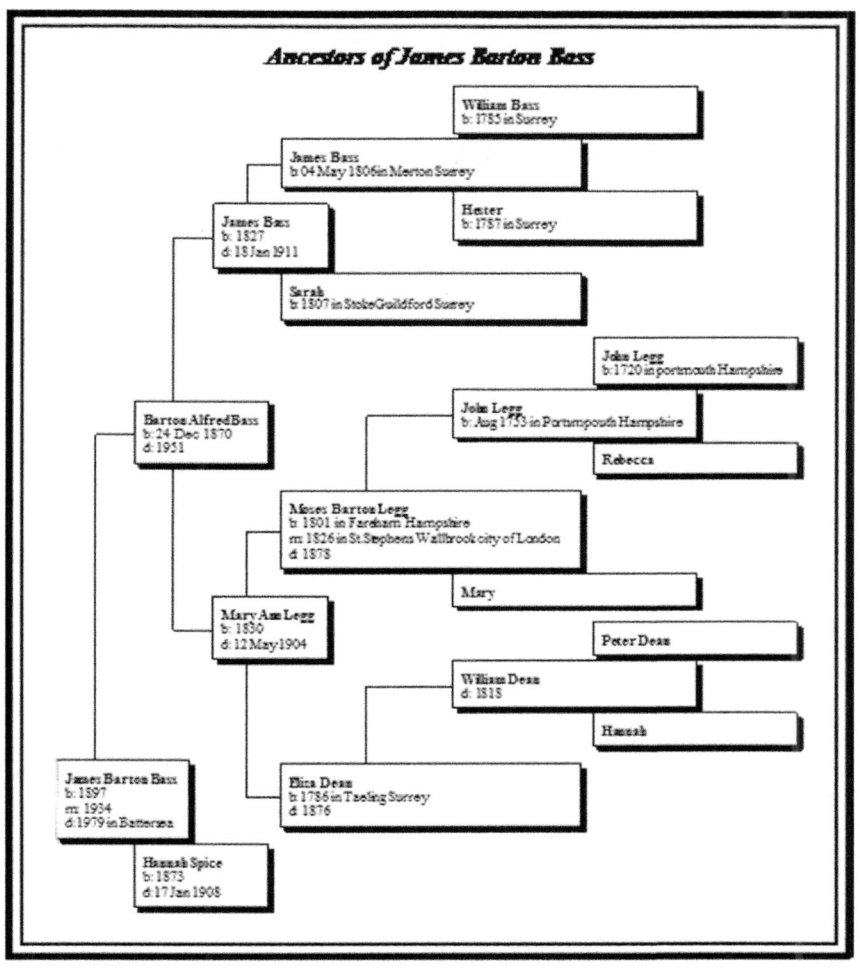

Ancestors of James Barton Bass

William Bass
b: 1785 in Surrey

James Bass
b: 04 May 1806 in Merton Surrey

Hester
b: 1787 in Surrey

James Bass
b: 1827
d: 18 Jan 1911

Sarah
b: 1807 in Stoke Guildford Surrey

John Legg
b: 1720 in portsmouth Hampshire

John Legg
b: Aug 1753 in Portsmouth Hampshire

Rebecca

Barton Alfred Bass
b: 24 Dec 1870
d: 1951

Moses Barton Legg
b: 1801 in Fareham Hampshire
m: 1826 in St.Stephens Wallbrook city of London
d: 1878

Mary

Mary Ann Legg
b: 1830
d: 12 May 1904

Peter Dean

William Dean
d: 1818

Hannah

James Barton Bass
b: 1897
m: 1934
d: 1979 in Battersea

Eliza Dean
b: 1786 in Taeling Surrey
d: 1876

Hannah Spice
b: 1873
d: 17 Jan 1908

MAY 1915
A young James Barton Bass aged 17 years 11 months

**James Bass, (in the centre is probably Harry Norcott)
The INNOCENTS – August 1915 at Hurst Park Racecourse**

Shrapnel wound, right groin – September 1916

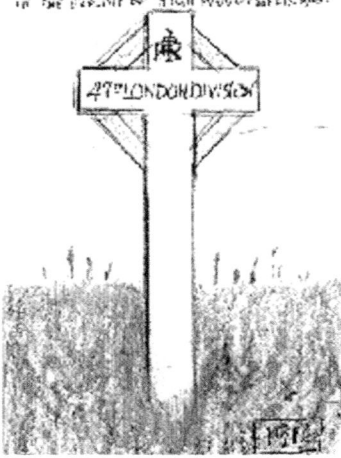

by James Bass

View towards Bridge at Hill 60 - 1916 by J Bass

View towards Bridge at Hill 60 - 2006

William George Mayfield & his father Joseph Mayfield – 1914

J Bass - June 1917 - 20th birthday

James Bass October 1917

BOURLON WOODS MEMORIAL – 2007

**Envelope of a letter returned to James
Bass's father, stamped 'missing'**

Army Form B. 104—83.

No. _____

(In replying, please quote above No.)

Infantry Record Office _____ Record Office,

4 LONDON WALL Bldgs. _____

_____ Station.

JAN 1 1 '18 E.C. 2 _____ 191

Sir,

I regret to have to inform you that a report has this day been received from the War Office to the effect that (No.) *322103* (Rank) *Rfmn* (Name) *J B Baso* (Regiment) ~~6TH LONDON REGT~~ was

Strike out part which does not apply.

[~~reported as "missing" after~~ | ~~taken prisoner during~~] the engagement at _____

on the *20 Novr 1917*

Should he subsequently rejoin, or any other information be received concerning him, such information will be at once communicated to you.

I am,

Sir,

Your obedient Servant,

[signature] Col

I/C INFANTRY RECORD OFFICE

Officer in charge of Records.

LONDON

Post card issued to POW

Arthur Baines Loyal North Lancashire Regiment

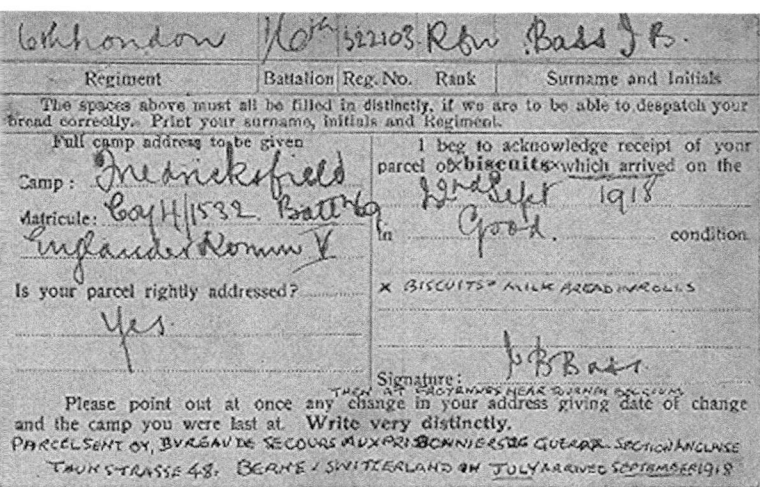

Receipt card for Red Cross Parcel

Arthur

Froggy   Cook   James Schmidt

2nd Row   2nd Row

Conde

Anna Van Dael

**Anna Van Dael
& 2 Belgian soldiers**

Arthur & James - Dec 1918

Anna, Arthur & James - Nov 1918

'The Lookout' 1929

Grand opening of the 'Lookout' 1929. James Bass

Inspection by Sir Joseph Hood outside the 'Lookout'. James Bass

Our old Standard approaches the altar to be " Laid-Up ". Standard Bearer Mr. J. B. Bass. Escorts:— Mr. C. V. Amor, Mr. W. G. Sparks, M.M. All 1914-18

James Bass Carrying the Standard.

Printed in Great
Britain
by Amazon